BIBLE CURIOSITIES

PAUL KENT & TRACY M. SUMNER

BIBLE

PAUL KENT & TRACY M. SUMNER

CURIOSITIES

AN ILLUSTRATED **GUIDE** *to the*
MYSTERIOUS, ODD & **SHOCKING**
STORIES *of* **SCRIPTURE**

BARBOUR
PUBLISHING

Bible story text by Paul Kent, previously published as *Bible Marvels, Oddities, and Shockers*. Sidebar material written and compiled by Tracy M. Sumner.

Print ISBN 978-1-62416-633-4

Cover image © Greg Jackson, Thinkpen Design

Published by Barbour Publishing, Inc., P.O. Box 719, Uhrichsville, Ohio 44683, www.barbourbooks.com

Our mission is to publish and distribute inspirational products offering exceptional value and biblical encouragement to the masses.

Member of the
Evangelical Christian
Publishers Association

CONTENTS

INTRODUCTION

WARNING: THIS BOOK MAY CHANGE THE WAY YOU VIEW THE BIBLE

In a good way, of course. Because *Bible Curiosities* is written to bring the Bible to life, by introducing you to some of the most unusual, intriguing, and downright bizarre people and events in scripture.

No doubt you already know some of them—Noah and his ark, Solomon and his wives, Samson and his muscles. But it's a good bet there are stories here you're much less familiar with—of the Bible's *other* Noah, of time standing still, of the gruesome deaths of Abimelech, Jezebel, and King Herod.

In the pages to follow, you'll find some real head-scratchers. . .a few rib-ticklers. . .and quite a few stomach-turners. Yes, the Bible's that kind of book. There's fascinating stuff all through the scripture, if you can get past those long lists of "begats" and the very detailed rules on handling mildew in your house. (If you really need to know, that's in Leviticus 14.)

If you haven't already guessed, we'll be having some fun with these Bible stories. But don't mistake mirth for disrespect—the authors' bedrock belief is that every word of scripture is true, preserved by God Himself for an important purpose. As the apostle Paul once wrote to Christians in Rome, "Everything that was written in the past was written to teach us."

When Paul says "everything," he means *everything*—even the weird, the gross, and the "I-have-a-really-hard-time-believing-that." Whether we understand every story in the Bible, this book takes the position that they're totally true and completely trustworthy.

Before each of the nearly sixty entries, you'll find a list of Bible references from which the story is drawn. Unless otherwise noted, direct quotations are taken verbatim from the New International Version of the Bible, unless the context clearly indicates that the quote is the author's speculation. Facts presented have clear Bible support, unless they're so silly as to imply an obvious joke. (For example, "Welcome to Emerod City" has the victorious Philistine army taking a hot bubble bath and going to bed. C'mon, you wouldn't think *that's* in the Bible, would you?)

You're welcomed, even encouraged, to look up these stories in your own Bible. Ultimately, that's what this book is all about—getting people into God's Word. Read it for the fun and fascinating stories you'll find. . .and, along the way, you might just meet your Maker. No, wait—that doesn't sound right. How about this: Along the way, you might just get to know God Himself a little better. And what could be better than that?

So, without any further ado, we raise the curtain on *Bible Curiosities: An Illustrated Guide to the Mysterious, Odd, and Shocking Stories of Scripture.* . . .

PAUL KENT
TRACY M. SUMNER

MIRACLE MAN

SCRIPTURES REFERENCED:

JOHN 2:1–11; MATTHEW 14:13–21; MATTHEW 15:29–38; MATTHEW 21:18–22; MATTHEW 14:22–32; MARK 4:35–41; LUKE 8:1–3; MATTHEW 8:3; LUKE 8:40–48; MARK 8:22–26; MATTHEW 8:14–17; MATTHEW 4:23; JOHN 20:31; MARK 5:21–43; LUKE 7:11–17; JOHN 11:1–44; JOHN 2:19; ROMANS 1:4; JOHN 21:25

Many people in the Bible performed miracles, but none quite like Jesus. Who better to christen our journey than Christ Himself?

ONE AFTER ANOTHER. . .

Shortly after calling His first disciples, Jesus performed His first miracle—a bit of liquid alchemy that changed ordinary water into some mighty fine wine. This wedding present in Cana of Galilee duly impressed His new disciples, who "believed in him."

From that time on, Jesus' miracles multiplied like the few loaves and fishes He used to feed crowds of four and five thousand men—not including women and children (see "There *Is* Such a Thing as a Free Lunch" on page 72). For example, Jesus

- cursed a barren fig tree, and it immediately withered;
- walked on the waters of a stormy sea—and caused Peter to do the same, albeit briefly;
- calmed a storm with three words ("Quiet! Be still!"), stunning even the disciples who'd already seen Him do some pretty amazing things;
- drove demons out of many people, including His good friend Mary Magdalene, who helped to support Jesus financially;
- healed leprosy, paralysis, bleeding, blindness, fever, pain, epilepsy— in Matthew's words, "every disease and sickness among the people."

A fig tree bearing fruit. One time, when Jesus found a fig tree without figs, He said, "May you never bear fruit again!" (Matthew 21:19). When the tree promptly withered away, Jesus used the incident to teach His disciples the power of faith.

TWENTY-FIVE MIRACLES PERFORMED BY JESUS

- Heals Peter's mother-in-law (Matthew 8:14–15)
- Gives sight to two blind men (Matthew 9:27–31)
- Feeds four thousand with a few fish and seven loaves of bread (Matthew 15:32–38)
- Heals man's withered hand (Matthew 12:10)
- Walks on the water (Matthew 14:25)
- Heals demoniac at Capernaum synagogue (Mark 1:23–26)
- Calms a violent storm (Mark 4:37–39)
- Heals Gadarene demoniac (Mark 5:1–20)
- Raises Jairus's daughter from the dead (Mark 5:21–43)
- Heals Syrophoenician woman's daughter (Mark 7:24–30)
- Heals a deaf and dumb man (Mark 7:31–37)
- Gives blind man of Bethsaida sight (Mark 8:22–26)
- Heals lunatic child (Mark 9:14–29)
- Gives sight to Bartimaeus (Mark 10:46–52)
- Arranges a miraculous catch of fish (Luke 5:4–11)
- Heals a centurion's servant (Luke 7:1–10)
- Raises a widow's son from the dead (Luke 7:11–17)
- Heals woman with issue of blood (Luke 8:43–48)
- Heals blind and dumb demoniac (Luke 11:14)
- Heals ten lepers (Luke 17:11–19)
- Turns water into wine at wedding in Cana (John 2:1–11)
- Cures nobleman's son in Capernaum (John 4:46–54)
- Heals man at Bethsaida (John 5:1–9)
- Gives sight to the man born blind (John 9:1–7)
- Raises Lazarus from the dead (John 11:38–44)

YOU THINK THAT'S COOL?
GET A LOAD OF THIS. . .

Jesus' good friend John said he wrote down the amazing miracles of Jesus' ministry so that you, as his reader, "may believe that Jesus is the Messiah, the Son of God, and that by believing you may have life in his name." But just in case all those healings, exorcisms, and examples of control over nature weren't impressive enough for everyone, Jesus could also step up the power a notch—by actually raising people from the dead.

- There was the twelve-year-old daughter of a Galilean synagogue ruler named Jairus. Jesus held her by the hand and commanded, "Little girl, I say to you, get up!" She did—to the utter amazement of her friends and family, who had gathered for a funeral but left with notes of celebration ringing in their ears.
- There was the young son of a widow in Nain. He popped out of his coffin at Jesus' command, "Young man, I say to you, get up!" Onlookers were, once again, stunned.
- There was Jesus' good friend Lazarus, who'd been in a tomb for quite a while before Jesus appeared. "Lord," said Lazarus's sister Martha, "by this time there is a bad odor, for he has been there four days." But why would a little decomposition interfere with Jesus' work? He had put all those molecules together in the first place. "Lazarus, come out!" Jesus shouted—and out of the tomb walked the mummy, "wrapped with strips of linen, and a cloth around his face." No big deal to Jesus, who said simply, "Take off the grave clothes and let him go."

Lazarus probably wasn't quite as mummified as this Egyptian example. . . but he'd definitely been dead and in the grave for four days when Jesus called him back to life. No word on Lazarus's reaction, but "many of the Jews who had come to visit Mary [Lazarus's sister], and had seen what Jesus did, believed in him" (John 11:45).

What *was* a big deal was the time Jesus brought *Himself* back to life—just as He'd predicted. "Destroy this temple," Jesus said of His body to a group of antagonistic Jews, "and I will raise it again in three days."

That's exactly what He did, reviving Himself and zapping miraculously through the solid rock of a sealed tomb (see "Successful Teleportation" on page 120). By that spectacular feat, Jesus "was appointed the Son of God in power."

APPROXIMATE DATES IN THE LIFE OF JESUS

- 4 or 5 BC—His Birth
- 4 or 5 BC —Journey to Egypt with His Family
- 3 or 4 BC —Return from Egypt
- AD 8—Boyhood Visit to the Temple
- AD 26—The Ministry of John the Baptist
- AD 26—Baptized by John the Baptist
- AD 26—First Year of His Ministry (Year of Inauguration)
- AD 27—Second Year of His Ministry (Year of Popularity)
- AD 28—Third Year of His Ministry (Year of Opposition)
- AD 29 or 30—Year of His Death

Nobody can say for sure what Jesus looked like, but this old orthodox icon shows the common perception of Him.

NOT THE END OF THE STORY

Though the four Gospels give several dozen examples of Jesus' amazing doings, the apostle John indicated that those accounts may be only the tip of a miracle iceberg. The last verse of John's Gospel says, "If every one of them were written down, I suppose that even the whole world would not have room for the books that would be written."

Yeah, Jesus was really a miracle man. Or maybe we should say, "Jesus *is* a miracle man." He's still working wonders today in the lives of all who choose to follow Him.

The Library of Congress in Washington DC is the largest library in the world, said to contain approximately 15 million books, thirty-nine million manuscripts, thirteen million photographs, and four million maps—among other things. And, according to the apostle John, all that information would only scratch the surface of Jesus' doings (John 21:25)!

MIRACLE MAN 2

SCRIPTURES REFERENCED:

2 KINGS 2–6; 2 KINGS 13:20–21; LUKE 4:14–30

f we were awarding Olympic medals to biblical miracle workers, Jesus would clearly take the gold. In sheer numbers of miracles and their impact on people—both then and now—Jesus' amazing feats overshadow those of everyone else in scripture.

But there's a strong candidate for the second-place silver—the Old Testament prophet Elisha.

VARIETY AND VOLUME

Like the mythical King Midas, whose touch turned everything to gold, Elisha seemed to work a miracle wherever he went. You want examples? How about this list—abridged, mind you:

- dividing the Jordan River with Elijah's cloak
- healing a poison stream
- purifying a tainted gourd stew
- multiplying a widow's cooking oil
- feeding one hundred hungry men with twenty loaves of bread (that's the opening image by the Italian master Tintoretto)
- curing a military commander's leprosy
- raising a young man from the dead

The Jordan isn't a huge river, as rivers go. . .but try parting it with a fleet of bulldozers, let alone a cloak!

Even with the wooden handle attached, that ax head isn't going to float—unless there's a miracle-working prophet nearby. Cue Elisha. . .

With some oddball situations like making an ax head float and blinding an enemy army thrown in for good measure, Elisha's miracles are like a two-pound bag of M&M's—a lot to chew on, in many different hues. (You can find more details on many of these miracles in "Prophet Breaks the Law—of Physics" on page 146 and "The Free Lunch Preview" on page 78.)

EVER HEARD OF THIS ONE?

But there's another Elisha marvel so amazing it might be called a bizarrity. (No, that's not really a word—but maybe if you start using it, we'll get it into the dictionary someday.)

Here's how the Bible records it:

> *Elisha died and was buried. Now Moabite raiders used to enter the country every spring. Once while some Israelites were burying a man, suddenly they saw a band of raiders; so they threw the man's body into Elisha's tomb. When the body touched Elisha's bones, the man came to life and stood up on his feet.*

Elisha didn't even have to be *alive* to perform miracles. That's good for at least second place in our little Olympic competition, isn't it?

Elisha was in this condition when he performed his final miracle—restoring life to a dead body tossed into the tomb where Elisha's bones rested. Read the whole story in 2 Kings 13:20–21.

I'M STILL SHAKING MY HEAD. . .

One striking fact about this miracle is the offhanded way the author of 2 Kings approaches it: The two verses quoted earlier constitute the entire biblical record of this marvel. And, apart from a brief comment by Jesus as recorded by Luke, these verses represent the final scriptural reference to Elisha.

It almost seems that Elisha's miracles were so common they'd become ho-hum—even a posthumous miracle, to the point of raising a dead man to life, merited only the briefest of mentions in the Bible.

Or perhaps there's a lesson here for us. Though the miracle is important enough to be noted, maybe we're not supposed to put our focus on the event or the prophet behind it. Perhaps our excitement and enthusiasm should be reserved for the God who powers those miracles.

HAVING THE NERVE TO ASK FOR "MORE"

As Elisha entered the city of Bethel with his mentor Elijah, he knew it wouldn't be long before God took his friend away to heaven. He also knew he had some big shoes to fill. He knew Elijah as an amazing prophet of God and miracle worker who had a showdown with the priests of Baal that proved that the Lord was God.

After the two men left Bethel and crossed the Jordan River (after Elijah had parted the water by striking it with his mantle), Elijah asked his disciple, "Tell me, what can I do for you before I am taken from you?" (2 Kings 2:9).

Elisha didn't hesitate in answering but blurted out, "Let me inherit a double portion of your spirit" (2 Kings 2:9).

Elisha saw Elijah carried up to heaven on a whirlwind of fire and immediately received a double portion of his spirit, just as he had requested. Elisha performed many miracles—he healed a polluted water source for the people of Jericho, provided oil for a widow, and caused a "great woman" of Shunem to have a child then brought him back to life after he died. He fed a hundred people from twenty loaves of bread. At Elisha's command, Naaman, captain of the Syrian king, bathed in the Jordan and was healed of leprosy.

WHATEVER HAPPENED TO. . .THE GOLDEN CALF?

SCRIPTURES REFERENCED:
EXODUS 19–32; EXODUS 12:35–36

t's not unusual to find ancient Middle Eastern calf statues in museums around the world. But what about the Bible's "golden calf," fashioned as a false god for the people of Israel by Moses' brother Aaron? You'll *never* see that one—Moses made sure of it.

DUMB AND DUMBER

The CliffsNotes version of the golden calf goes like this: Three months after they broke out of slavery in Egypt (thanks to a string of ten miraculous plagues that fell on the pharaoh and his people), the Israelites arrived in the Sinai Desert. There, God gave Moses a message to share with the people. They were God's "treasured possession. . .a kingdom of priests and a holy nation." Thus affirmed, the people replied to Moses, "We will do everything the LORD has said."

As a popular saying from a few years ago went, *"Not!"* The Israelites would, within six weeks, be reveling in the wild worship of a metal moo-er.

Moses went up Mount Sinai to receive the Ten Commandments—and a whole bunch of other rules and regulations—from God Himself. As Moses' stay grew longer and longer (ultimately, he'd spend forty days and forty nights on the mountain), the Israelites got itchy.

> *When the people saw that Moses was so long in coming down from the mountain, they gathered around Aaron and said, "Come, make us gods who will go before us. As for this fellow Moses who brought us up out of Egypt, we don't know what has happened to him."*

Dumb idea. But Aaron's response was even dumber.

Moses' spokesman, who'd personally seen God bodyslam the Egyptians in springing the Israelites from bondage, asked the people for their golden earrings—many of which had likely been given to them by Egyptian people during the Exodus itself. Then Aaron formed the accumulated gold into a calf and announced, "These are your gods, Israel, who brought you up out of Egypt."

After that, the people began sacrificing burnt offerings to the idol and "sat down to eat and drink and got up to indulge in revelry."

Modern tourists stop at the base of Mount Sinai. Four thousand years earlier, this was the site of one of the Bible's more dramatic screwups.

THE PARTY'S OVER

God, of course, knew what was happening—and He was none too pleased. The first rule He'd given Moses to forward to the people was this: "You shall have no other gods before me."

The Lord suggested destroying the Israelites and making Moses the forefather of a new nation—but Moses begged God to reconsider. "Why should the Egyptians say, 'It was with evil intent that he brought them out, to kill them in the mountains and to wipe them off the face of the earth'? . . . Remember your servants Abraham, Isaac and Israel, to whom you swore by your own self: 'I will make your descendants as numerous as the stars in the sky and I will give your descendants all this land I promised them, and it will be their inheritance forever.'"

God relented, but the Israelites still had to face the wrath of Moses. Marching down Mount Sinai with the stone tablets of the Ten Commandments in his arms, his second-in-command, Joshua, at his side, and the sound of the Israelites' merrymaking ringing in his ears, Moses prepared for a confrontation with his older brother.

When he saw the golden idol and the people dancing around it, Moses threw down the stone tablets, which shattered at his feet. (Yes, it was just like Charlton Heston in the movie version.) And Moses grabbed Aaron by the figurative lapels, asking incredulously, "What did these people do to you, that you led them into such great sin?"

BYE-BYE, GOLDEN CALF

Aaron spluttered some lame-o excuse ("They gave me the gold, and I threw it into the fire, and out came this calf!"), but not before Moses took decisive action. His three-step plan ensured that no one would try to worship this particular idol ever again.

First, Moses burned the calf in a fire. Gold melts, so before long the calf was looking rather uncalflike—more just a blob of shiny yellow metal.

Next, Moses ground the gold into powder. If anyone had thoughts of gathering up the gold to re-create the calf idol, this step made such a plan highly unlikely.

"Unlikely" became "impossible" after Moses' final move. He took the powder, scattering it over water—and then made the people of Israel *drink* it. So that's what happened to the golden calf.

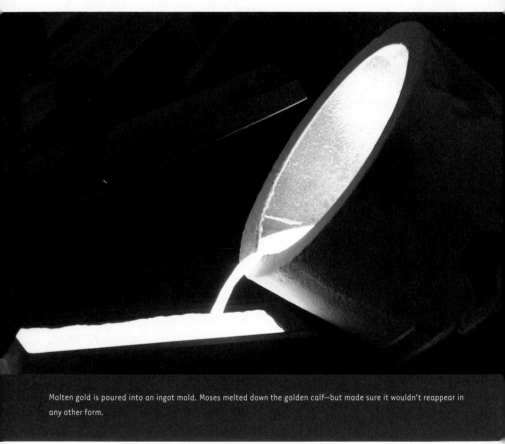

Molten gold is poured into an ingot mold. Moses melted down the golden calf—but made sure it wouldn't reappear in any other form.

NOT QUITE THE END OF THE STORY

Even though the idol was gone, the idea remained—and, sadly, would pop up again years later when Solomon's kingdom split into northern and southern segments. The northern kingdom of Israel (as opposed to the southern kingdom, which called itself Judah) would launch itself with calf worship and never entirely give it up.

They say you can't keep a good man down. Apparently, that's also true of a bad idea.

MORE ABOUT MOSES

- Family—Father Amram, mother Jochebed (Exodus 6:20); from the tribe of Levi (Exodus 2:1); brother Aaron (Exodus 4:14) and sister Miriam (Exodus 15:20).
- Early life (Exodus 2:2–10)—His birth; hidden in the reeds, adopted by king's daughter, and named Moses
- Youth and adulthood (Exodus 2:11–15)—Kills an Egyptian and flees to Midian
- At Midian (Exodus 2:16–25)—Marries Zipporah, a priest's daughter
- God's call—(Exodus 3:1–4:16)— Moses sees burning bush and hears God's call but makes excuses; God promises divine and human help
- Return to Egypt (Exodus 4:29–12:29)—Demands that a stubborn Pharaoh free the people of Israel; God sends plagues; the Passover established; Pharaoh frees Israelites
- The Exodus from Egypt (Exodus 12:30–18:27)—Pharaoh pursues the Israelites; the crossing of the Red Sea; the Song of Moses; God provides for the Israelites
- At Mount Sinai (Exodus 19–40)— Moses ascends the mountain three times and makes covenant with God; receives the Ten Commandments and the rest of the Law; the golden calf

- Journey from Sinai to Kadesh Barnea (Numbers 10:11–12:15)—The pillar of cloud; the people complain; seventy elders appointed
- At Kadesh Barnea (Numbers 13:26–14:45)—The spies' report on the Promised Land; the people rebel, resulting in God's wrath; Amelek defeats Israel
- Forty years in the wilderness (Numbers 14:33–16:50)—God declares the people would wander; rebellion breaks out
- Return to Kadesh Barnea (Numbers 20:1–13)—The death of Miriam, Moses' sister; the people complain over lack of water; Moses' sin
- Journey to the Jordan River (Numbers 20:14–33:49)—The death of Aaron; the fiery serpents; the story of Balaam
- Moses' final days (Deuteronomy 32:1–34:6)—Moses' farewell address and blessing; Moses views Promised Land; Moses' death
- Appearance at the Transfiguration (Matthew 17:2–3)—Moses and Elijah appear at Jesus' transfiguration

MAN MARRIES 700 WOMEN

SCRIPTURES REFERENCED:
1 KINGS 11:1–25; 1 SAMUEL 13:13–14; 1 KINGS 3:1–28, 1 KINGS 12; ECCLESIASTES
1:1–2; ECCLESIASTES 2:8; ECCLESIASTES 12:13

Any husband or wife, speaking honestly, will tell you that marriage isn't easy. It takes hard work to mold two distinct personalities into a unified whole and to deal with all the other challenges a couple faces—including in-laws.

So why on earth would a man want *seven hundred* wives?

A GOOD BEGINNING

You'll find such a man in the pages of the Bible. Not surprisingly, he was a wealthy and powerful king. Quite surprisingly, he was known as the world's *wisest* person.

If you hadn't already figured it out, the man was Solomon, the third king in Israel's history. He took the throne of his father, David, the "man after [God's] own heart" who led the cantankerous, often idolatrous Israelites to their greatest heights as a nation. As Solomon stepped into this situation, God made him an amazing offer: "Ask for whatever you want me to give you." From this divine smorgasbord, Solomon was smart enough to choose wisdom. "I am only a little child and do not know how to carry out my duties," the novice ruler told God. "So give

Young Solomon, newly crowned as king, in his wiser days. When God offered to give Solomon anything he wanted, his request was for wisdom. Money and fame came as a side benefit. The painting is from the fifteenth century.

your servant a discerning heart to govern your people and to distinguish between right and wrong." God was pleased with Solomon's request and gave him not only great wisdom, but wealth and honor, too.

WISDOM ON PARADE

Almost immediately, Solomon's legendary wisdom was put to the test. Two prostitute roommates came to the king with an argument. The unsavory women had each gotten pregnant around the same time and each had had a baby boy. The babies slept in their mothers' beds at night.

One evening, one of the prostitutes rolled over in her sleep and smothered her son. When she realized what had happened, she hatched a cold, calculated plan: she quietly took her dead baby and gently laid it beside her roommate, then took the live baby into her own bed. When her roommate woke up to a dead son that wasn't hers, the argument began: "The living one is my son; the dead one is yours." "No! The dead one is yours; the living one is mine." Their quarrel made it all the way to the king's palace.

Solomon quickly got to the heart of the problem. "Bring me a sword," he commanded, then ordered his servants to cut the living baby in half. If both women wanted the boy, they'd each get at least part of their wish.

One of the prostitutes was happy with the plan; the other was horrified. "Please, my lord," she sobbed, "give her the living baby! Don't kill him!" That response told Solomon exactly who the real mother was, and the people of Israel were awed by his judgment.

Too bad he lost it along the way.

STANDIN' ON THE CORNER, WATCHIN' ALL THE GIRLS GO BY

Early on in his kingship, Solomon married the princess of Egypt. It was a political marriage made to seal an alliance with the pharaoh. There were many more such women to come—several hundred in all, but who's counting?

King Solomon "loved many foreign women besides Pharaoh's daughter—Moabites, Ammonites, Edomites, Sidonians, and Hittites. They were from nations about which the LORD had told the Israelites, 'You must not intermarry with them, because they will surely turn your hearts after their gods.' "

But Solomon didn't care. He let his emotions overwhelm his intellect, and he collected wives the way people today amass Beanie Babies or baseball cards. In the end, Solomon had seven hundred wives, plus three hundred

TWELVE IMPORTANT MARRIED COUPLES OF SCRIPTURE

- Abraham and Sarah
- Adam and Eve
- Boaz and Ruth
- Joseph and Mary
- Zacharias and Elisabeth
- Isaac and Rebekah
- Ananias and Sapphira
- Jacob and Rachel
- Elkanah and Hannah
- David and Bathsheba
- Ahab and Jezebel
- Aquila and Priscilla

The traditional marriage vow includes the line, "For better or for worse." Many biblical marriages were for the better; some were definitely for the worst.

concubines—wives in every way except for the wedding ceremony. And God's warning (no surprise here) was proven true.

Solomon's wives "led him astray," as the writer of the Bible's first book of Kings put it. "As Solomon grew old, his wives turned his heart after other gods, and his heart was not fully devoted to the LORD his God. . . . He followed Ashtoreth the goddess of the Sidonians, and Molech the detestable god of the Ammonites. So Solomon did evil in the eyes of the LORD; he did not follow the LORD completely, as David his father had done."

Wisdom? Solomon had all the wisdom of God at his disposal. The problem was that he didn't use it.

According to the "World Record Academy," a Dusseldorf, Germany, woman has amassed the largest Barbie doll collection, with more than 6,000. Solomon didn't have quite that many wives—"only" seven hundred—but they didn't just sit on display somewhere, either. Sadly, they turned him to false gods.

TRUTH *AND* CONSEQUENCES

Sin always brings punishment, and Solomon soon was under the combined weight of his thousand idol-worshipping women. God raised up enemies to punish Solomon—an Edomite named Hadad, nursing a long-standing grudge against the Israelites, who had killed all of his male relatives during David's time; a rebel from Zobah named Rezon, who ruled in the area of modern-day Syria and "was hostile toward Israel"; and one of Solomon's own officials, Jeroboam, who was told by God Himself (through the prophet Ahijah) that he would rule ten of Israel's twelve tribes, snatched away from the womanizing king.

Solomon didn't actually see that day. After trying unsuccessfully to kill Jeroboam, who snuck off to Egypt and hid, Solomon died after ruling Israel forty years. His kingdom began to disintegrate, as Jeroboam returned

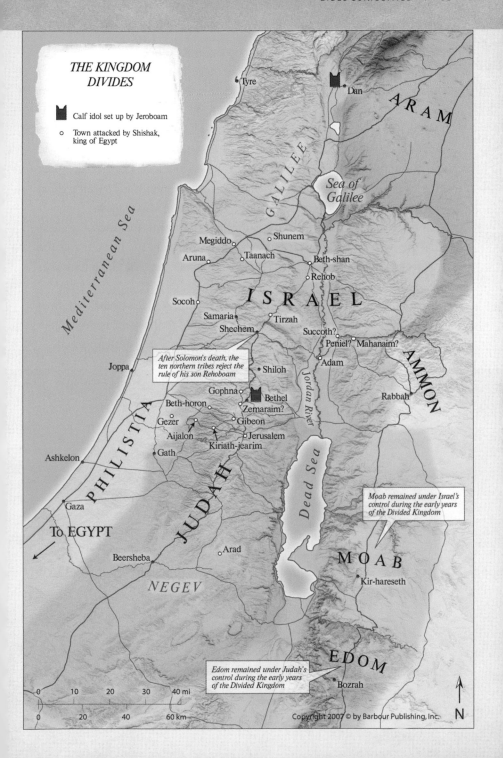

THE KINGDOM DIVIDES

▮ Calf idol set up by Jeroboam

○ Town attacked by Shishak, king of Egypt

Tyre

Dan

ARAM

Sea of Galilee

GALILEE

Mediterranean Sea

Megiddo

Shunem

Aruna

Taanach

Beth-shan

Rehob

Socoh

ISRAEL

Samaria

Tirzah

Shechem

Succoth?

Peniel? Mahanaim?

Joppa

After Solomon's death, the ten northern tribes reject the rule of his son Rehoboam

Adam

AMMON

Shiloh

Jordan River

Gophna

Rabbah

Beth-horon

Bethel

Zemaraim?

Gezer

Gibeon

Aijalon

Jerusalem

Kiriath-jearim

Ashkelon

PHILISTIA

Gath

JUDAH

Dead Sea

Moab remained under Israel's control during the early years of the Divided Kingdom

Gaza

To EGYPT

Beersheba

Arad

MOAB

NEGEV

Kir-hareseth

Edom remained under Judah's control during the early years of the Divided Kingdom

EDOM

Bozrah

| 0 | 10 | 20 | 30 | 40 mi |

| 0 | 20 | 40 | 60 km |

Copyright 2007 © by Barbour Publishing, Inc.

N

to rebel against the new king, Solomon's son Rehoboam. Generations of bad leadership followed, both in the northern kingdom of Israel (the ten tribes God offered to Jeroboam) and in the southern kingdom of Judah (two tribes God kept in Solomon's line, to fulfill his promises to David).

It was a depressing end to a kingship that started with great promise. But some Bible students think Solomon may have rediscovered his wisdom—at least some of it—in his latter days. The Bible's book of Ecclesiastes, they think, was penned by Solomon, who begins by lamenting, "Meaningless! Meaningless! . . . Utterly meaningless! Everything is meaningless."

All that *vanity*, to use the King James Version term, included the pleasures the man of Ecclesiastes chased: "silver and gold for myself, and the treasure of kings and provinces. . .male and female singers, and a harem as well." But none of those things made him happy.

Perhaps Solomon's great wisdom begins to reappear in the twelfth and final chapter of Ecclesiastes, where "the Teacher" comes to the conclusion that the whole duty of man is simply this: "Fear God and keep his commandments."

Solomon prays to dedicate the temple he built for God in Jerusalem. Solomon's father, David, had wanted to build a "house for the Name of the LORD my God," but God said no—because of David's reputation for shedding blood in war. Solomon, "a man of peace and rest," was God's choice as temple builder (see 1 Chronicles 22:2–10).

One of the under-appreciated miracles of the Bible is how—with all those wives—Solomon found any time for writing!

SOLOMON'S WORDS OF WISDOM

Son of King David and Bathsheba, Solomon was loved by God. Despite the efforts of his half brother Adonijah to take the throne, Solomon became king over Israel with the support of his father, David.

When God came to Solomon in a vision and asked what he wanted, the king requested "a discerning heart" to rule His people (1 Kings 3:9). Because Solomon asked wisely, God gave him wisdom, understanding, and the wealth and honor he had not requested. Solomon built the Lord's temple with the aid of Hiram, Tyre's king. Solomon dedicated the temple with a beautiful prayer and benediction (1 Kings 8:22–61).

While Solomon made more of his share of bad decisions during his monarchy, some of which led to the division of Israel into two kingdoms after his death, his words of wisdom are prominent in the Bible. Solomon is often credited with

- Psalms 72 and 127
- the first twenty-nine chapters of the Book of Proverbs (Agur and Lemuel wrote chapters 30 and 31)
- the Song of Solomon
- the book of Ecclesiastes
- maybe even the book of Job

EARTH STANDS STILL!

SCRIPTURES REFERENCED:
JOSHUA 10:1–15; JOSHUA 6:21; JOSHUA 9

Ever notice that we can always find time to complain about our lack of time? "I need more hours in my day" is a common refrain in twenty-first-century society. But thirty-five hundred years ago, the great Jewish leader Joshua voiced a similar wish—and got literally what he asked for.

JOSHUA: GOD'S HIT MAN

Joshua had a dirty job, but somebody had to do it. Assigned the task of cleansing the Promised Land of its idol-worshipping denizens, Joshua was under God's orders to wipe out everyone—"men and women, young and old." This had been the rule at Jericho, and Joshua had followed through.

Ten miles northwest of Jericho, Joshua led a similar slaughter at a town called Ai. Bad news, they say, travels fast—and leaders of other towns in the region started to sweat.

In Jerusalem, King Adoni-Zedek called on his fellow Amorite leaders in Hebron, Jarmuth, Lachish, and Eglon to join him in a military expedition against the town of Gibeon. The Gibeonites had made peace with Joshua by a clever ruse. Dressing up in old, worn-out clothes and carrying dry, moldy bread, men of Gibeon had approached the Israelite army claiming they had traveled a great distance. And, oh, by the way, they added, "Make a treaty with us."

In one of the few mistakes the great leader made, Joshua took the Gibeonites' word.

The sneaky Gibeonites were behind Joshua's only recorded boo-boo, when they dusted up their donkeys and put on a show of having traveled a great distance. They wanted Joshua to think they lived far away, so he wouldn't destroy them along with other people in the Promised Land. The trick worked, as Joshua made a treaty with them—but they ultimately became servants, "woodcutters and water carriers," for the Israelites (Joshua 9:27).

Without consulting God, the Israelites made a peace treaty with the "travelers"—and learned three days later that they actually lived all of eight miles away.

Now, with the armies of five Amorite kings bearing down on them, the Gibeonites called on their Israelite allies, and Joshua lived up to his promise: He sent his entire army to Gibeon. Though Joshua had been fooled by the Gibeonites, God hadn't been, and He used the unlikely alliance to move Joshua toward the ultimate goal. "Do not be afraid of them," God said of the five Amorite armies. "I have given them into your hand."

ANOTHER MIRACULOUS VICTORY

The Israelites' victory at Gibeon wasn't the only one they took under unusual—make that *miraculous*—circumstances. In fact, it wasn't even the first. Earlier, Joshua's men prepared to take Jericho, a Moabite city west of the Jordan River. The Israelites entered Canaan, crossing the Jordan River near Jericho, and camped in the Jericho plain as they conquered the Midianites. But then, God gave Joshua an unusual battle plan to take Jericho: For six consecutive days Israel's soldiers were to walk once around the city; on the seventh day they were to go around the city seven times, with the priests walking before the troops, blowing their trumpets and carrying the ark of the covenant. When the priests made a long blast, the people were to shout, and Jericho would be theirs. When the priests offered the trumpet blasts and the people shouted, the walls of the city came tumbling down, and the Israelites destroyed everything in the city—except for a prostitute named Rahab and her family (see Joshua 6).

Some of the Israelites themselves seem unsure of Joshua's "battle plan" for Jericho—to walk around the walled city with the ark of the covenant and trumpets. Actually, it wasn't Joshua's plan, it was God's—and it worked to perfection.

Here are the proverbial "golf ball–sized" hailstones. The Bible says God dropped "large hailstones" on the Amorite army, "and more of them died from the hail than were killed by the swords of the Israelites" (Joshua 10:11).

ALL IS FAIR IN LOVE AND WAR

After an overnight march, Joshua and his soldiers surprised and routed their enemies in an early morning attack at Gibeon. The Amorite armies scattered, and the Israelites chased them down in a lethal pursuit. Many who escaped the Israelite swords found themselves on the receiving end of giant hailstones, dropped with precision by the divine bombardier.

By about noon, there were still enemy soldiers to mop up, and the foresighted Joshua didn't want his daylight to run out before the job was done. So he prayed an amazing, audacious prayer: "Sun, stand still over Gibeon, and you, moon, over the Valley of Aijalon."

Incredibly, they did.

For the better part of a day, the sun halted in the middle of the sky, refusing to budge on its normal course westward. Or maybe we should say the earth stopped its otherwise inexorable turning, making it *appear* that the sun had come to a halt. However you explain it, Joshua got several more hours of daylight to accomplish his task.

In an example of biblical understatement, the author of the book of Joshua noted that "there has never been a day like it before or since." And that's a good thing, too. If it happened again, can you imagine trying to adjust all the world's clocks?

THE MYSTERIOUS DEATH OF JUDAS ISCARIOT

SCRIPTURES REFERENCED:
MATTHEW 27:1–5; ACTS 1:18–19; MATTHEW 26:14–16; JOHN 12:1–6

ha—a contradiction in the Bible! So say skeptics of the demise of Judas Iscariot.

The nefarious disciple, according to the Gospel of Matthew, hanged himself in remorse over his betrayal of Jesus. In Luke's book of Acts, Judas buys a field and, falling "headlong, his body burst open and all his intestines spilled out." So which is it?

SETTING THE STAGE

Either way, Judas had it coming. As one of the original twelve disciples, he—of all people—should have understood who Jesus was and what He was all about. But somehow Jesus' teachings, miracles, and examples of love, compassion, and faithfulness went right over Judas's head. Mr. Iscariot's main concern, it seemed, was money.

His deal with the chief priests, to hand Jesus over for thirty pieces of silver, wasn't the first example of Judas's lust for cold, hard cash. Another time, at the Bethany home of Mary, Martha, and Lazarus, Judas complained when Mary poured an expensive perfume on Jesus' feet. "Why wasn't this perfume sold and the money given to the poor?" he asked. "It was worth a year's wages."

Such a fine protest—from such a fraud. "He did not say this because he cared about the poor," wrote the apostle John, "but because he was a thief; as keeper of the money bag, he used to help himself to

The Bible doesn't say exactly what kind of coins Judas got for betraying Jesus, other than that they were silver. This silver roman coin dates to about two centuries after Judas's treachery.

what was put into it." Sounds like some of our twenty-first-century business scandals, huh?

Judas's far greater sin, of course, was the blatant sellout of his friend and teacher, Jesus. If there is any redeeming element to the story, it is that the betrayer did feel remorse—a remorse quickly followed by his own death. But was the death by hanging, or did Judas fall to the ground and crack open like an egg?

SOLVING THE PUZZLE

Perhaps the Acts account is less a contradiction than it is a *continuation* of Matthew's story. Matthew says Judas went to the temple to return his thirty coins to the chief priests and elders, then "went away and hanged himself." In Acts, the apostle Peter reports Judas's nasty collision with the earth on a field bought "with the payment he received for his wickedness."

Maybe the whole story is this: Judas threw his betrayal money at the feet of the religious leaders, then went out and hanged himself. At some point, Judas's rope either broke or was cut, and his body fell to the ground, split open, and "all his intestines spilled out." The chief priests and elders took the thirty silver coins and purchased the field in which Judas died, which the locals began calling *Akeldama*, the "Field of Blood." Peter, telling the story of Judas in Acts, spoke figuratively of Judas purchasing the field. Though the

THEY TOOK THEIR OWN LIVES. . .

The Bible records seven different men taking their own lives. They are

- Abimelek, the son of Gideon, who was proclaimed king after his father's death. He actually had assistance in his suicide, ordering his armor-bearer to kill him (Judges 9:50–54).
- Samson, judge of Israel (Judges 16:30).
- Saul, Israel's first monarch, after the Philistines defeated his army at Mount Gilboa. He died when he fell on his own sword (1 Samuel 31:1–4).
- Saul's armor-bearer, after he discovered that the king was dead (1 Samuel 31:5).
- Ahithophel, who deserted King David during Absalom's revolt. Like Judas, he hanged himself (2 Samuel 17:23).
- Zimri, who murdered Elah and succeeded him as king of Israel. His reign lasted only seven days. Omri, who had been elected as king, then laid siege to Tirzah. Zimri set fire to the palace and was burned to death (1 Kings 16:8–20).
- Judas Iscariot, who hanged himself after betraying Jesus (Matthew 27:5).

religious leaders actually bought the field, Judas "paid for it" with his life, the reward of his sin.

Mystery solved? Maybe. But that melancholy feeling remains.

Pottery fragments carry the names of Jewish defenders of Masada, the mountaintop fortress captured by the Roman army after a long siege. Some guess that the fragments were lots, drawn to decide who would kill whom to prevent capture by the enemy. Nearly a thousand Jews died on Masada.

FIRST THINGS FIRST

Following Jesus' return to heaven, the apostles would receive the Holy Spirit (Acts 2), and then they would begin their ministries in Jerusalem and then around the known world. It would be world-changing work empowered by a world-changing Holy Spirit.

But first, there was the matter of replacing Judas, who committed suicide after betraying Jesus. Judas's replacement was chosen at a meeting of about 120 of Jesus' followers in Jerusalem. The two candidates were men named Joseph (called Justus and also known as Barsabbas) and Matthias, whose name means "Gift of God." Both had been among Jesus' disciples (but not apostles) during His earthly ministry (Acts 1:21–22)

After praying over their decision, the assembly "cast lots" (Acts 1:26)— probably some ancient practice similar to flipping a coin or drawing a name out of a hat—and selected Matthias as the new twelfth apostle.

The apostle Matthias is not mentioned anywhere else in the Bible, but ancient church tradition holds that he was one of the seventy disciples Jesus sent out in Luke 10:1, that he preached in Judea, and that, like most of the other apostles, died a martyr.

THE BIBLE'S
TERMINATOR

SCRIPTURES REFERENCED:
JUDGES 13—16; 1 SAMUEL 17:1—11

E ven people who have never touched a Bible know a few things about
Samson: He had amazing strength, a gal-pal named Delilah, and a thing
about long hair—perhaps on his women, but definitely on himself.

RULES ARE MEANT TO BE FOLLOWED

Samson, you see, was a Nazirite. From the time his birth announcement hit
the streets—even before his conception, thanks to an angel messenger—
there were a few special rules for the future tough guy. One rule was that he
couldn't snip his locks. That was part of God's deal to make Samson a "judge"
of Israel. But there were no black robes,
powdered wigs, and quiet chambers
for this judge—he represented another
meaning of the word, namely, *deliverer*.
And this delivery boy would take on
the dreaded Philistines, those nasty
neighbors who would later produce
a nine-foot-tall, insult-hurling brute
named Goliath.

For twenty years, Samson waged a
one-man war against the Philistines,
a pagan nation oppressing God's chosen people. And in this conflict, we
uncover a Bible shocker: Samson was
an eleventh-century BC Terminator, a
virtual killing machine.

Statues of "Justice" are often found outside
courthouses, where modern judges interpret
and apply laws. But in Samson's time, a judge
was a military leader, one who dispensed justice
in combat.

Sweet, juicy grapes were off the menu for Nazirites—as a sign of their separation from the world, to God.

WHAT IN THE WORLD IS A NAZIRITE?

The word *Nazirite* (or *Nazarite*) comes from a Hebrew word meaning "separated" or "consecrated." A Nazirite was someone who was separated from the general Hebrew population and devoted completely to God.

The conditions of the Nazirite vow are found in Numbers 6:1–8. In that passage, God directs Moses to tell the Israelites that anyone who wants (it was voluntary and open to men and women alike) to make this special vow

- Must abstain from consumption of alcohol and from any products of the grapevine, including vinegar, grape juice, grapes, grape seeds, grape skins, and raisins (verses 3–4)
- Must not cut their hair but let it grow long (verse 5)
- Must not touch or even go near a dead body, even that of a close family member (verses 6–7).

Nazirite vows were usually kept for about one to three months, but Samson was a Nazirite from the time of his birth until his death (Judges 13:7). At the end of the period of the vow, the Nazirite was required to burn his shaven hair and present specific offerings to the Lord (see Numbers 6:10–21).

PREP THE BODY BAGS

The man with the mane notched his first victory against another maned creature—a lion that attacked Samson as he went to see his Philistine girlfriend. (Yeah, his first filly was a Phillie—it was part of God's plan.) Samson killed the lion with his bare hands, kicking off a career of mayhem and destruction that truly boggles the mind.

Shortly afterward, during the happy couple's wedding festivities, Samson cockily posed a riddle to his thirty Philistine groomsmen. The question related to the lion Samson had killed, in which some bees had built a nest and started cranking out honey: "Out of the eater, something to eat; out of the strong, something sweet." Whoever won this little competition would get thirty sets of clothing from the losing side.

Samson's groomsmen didn't know about the lion, and the riddle made about as much sense as an Old Navy commercial. So they threatened the family of the future Mrs. Samson to get the answer. For the seven days of the wedding celebration, the poor woman cried—until Samson couldn't take it any longer. He told her the answer, she told the groomsmen, and they dutifully answered Samson's riddle. Though Samson knew he'd been cheated, he had honor enough to pay off his debt—but got the thirty changes of clothes from thirty guys in a nearby town, slaughtered for their threads. Terminator running total: 1 lion, 30 Philistines.

When Samson left the wedding, his future father-in-law didn't expect him to return—so he married off his daughter to the best man. Like a boomerang, Samson did come back, looking for his "wife." Learning she now belonged to another, he exacted revenge by capturing 300 foxes, tying them together in pairs with a lit torch between them, and setting them loose in the Philistines' grain

"King of the jungle," he's called, and with good reason. But a young lion was no match for Samson, when "the Spirit of the LORD came powerfully upon him so that he tore the lion apart with his bare hands as he might have torn a young goat" (Judges 14:6).

fields, vineyards, and olive groves. This bit of destruction begged another, so the Philistines killed Samson's woman and her father. Samson, in turn, slaughtered "many" Philistines in revenge. Terminator running total: 1 lion, up to 300 foxes, 30 plus "many" Philistines.

Some of Samson's own countrymen felt things were getting out of hand, and they asked their deliverer to let them deliver *him* into Philistine custody. Samson agreed, but once in his enemies' hands, "The Spirit of the LORD came powerfully upon him," and he grabbed the jawbone of a dead donkey, using it to kill 1,000 Philistines. Terminator running total: 1 lion, up to 300 foxes, 1,030 plus "many" Philistines.

TEMPLE OF DOOM

Samson's next known slaughter is his last recorded in the Bible. The seductive Delilah finally learned that rock-star hair was the secret of Samson's strength, and she found a barber to give him the ultimate buzz cut—while Samson slept, of course. All of his power now gone, Samson was captured, bound, blinded, and forced to grind grain in a Philistine prison.

Over time, stubble appeared on Samson's head. The stubble became fuzz, and the fuzz grew into a new 'do. The deliverer's strength began to grow, too, and when he got his chance, he exacted his final revenge on Israel's oppressors.

Called to the Philistine's pagan temple to perform for a massive crowd, Samson sensed his opportunity. During a break in the action, he leaned against a pillar, using his supernatural strength to push down the main supports. The temple itself was "crowded with men and women," not counting some 3,000 people on the roof. When the walls came tumbling down, potentially thousands more died in Samson's final act of "deliverance."

The Terminator's final body count: 1 lion, up to 300 foxes, 1,030 plus "many" plus several thousand Philistines—and Samson himself.

Without eyes, but with his long hair again, Samson exacts revenge on the Philistines, who had persecuted Israel and enslaved him personally. The event was in the 1100s BC; the woodcut is from the AD 1800s.

THE JUDGES OF ISRAEL

- Othniel (Judges 3:7–11)—Caleb's brother, Othniel delivered Israel from the king of Mesopotamia and judged Israel for forty years.
- Ehud (Judges 3:12–30)—The second judge of Israel who subdued the oppressing Moabites.
- Shamgar (Judges 3:31)—Fought bravely against the Philistines; killed six hundred Philistine soldiers with an ox goad.
- Deborah (Judges 4–5)—Israel's only female judge and prophetess, she held court under a palm tree. Deborah called Barak to lead warriors into battle against the Canaanite army commander, Sisera.
- Gideon (Judges 6–8)—The fifth judge of Israel, whom God raised up to lead his nation against the Midianites.
- Abimelek (Judges 9)—A son of Gideon, by his concubine. He killed all but one of his brothers and was made king of Shechem.
- Tola (Judges 10:1–2)—Judged Israel for twenty-three years.
- Jair (10:3–5)—The eighth judge of Israel, who led the nation for twenty-two years.
- Jephthah (Judges 10:6–12:7)—Eighth judge of Israel, Jephthah the Gileadite was Gilead's son by a prostitute.
- Elon (Judges 12:11–12)—Judged Israel for ten years.
- Abdon (Judges 12:13–15)—The twelfth judge of Israel who led the nation for eight years.
- Samson (Judges 13–16)—Twelfth judge of Israel, from the time of his conception he was supposed to follow a Nazirite vow.

- Eli (1 Samuel 4:18)—The high priest in Shiloh, where the ark of the covenant rested for a time. He rebuked Hannah for being drunk as she prayed for God to give her a child. Eli judged Israel forty years.
- Samuel (1 Samuel 7:15)—Samuel was born after his mother, Hannah, petitioned God to give her a child and promised to give him up to God's service in return. Samuel spoke out against the wickedness of Eli's sons. Samuel led the Israelites to repent of their idolatry, and he judged Israel for his whole life.

ANGELS: NOT CHUBBY KIDS WITH WINGS

SCRIPTURES REFERENCED:

JUDGES 6; LUKE 1:11–20; LUKE 2:8–9; MATTHEW 28:1–4; MATTHEW 2:13–14; ACTS 8:26–40; ACTS 10:3–6; REVELATION 22:8–9

hen did angels become so wimpy?

"Cute" is a good word for many angel images, especially those round-faced toddlers with little wing sprouts envisioned by the Renaissance artist Raphael. "Soft," "gentle," and "effeminate" might describe other angels in popular art.

But that's not the Bible way.

YIKES!

More often than not, angels scared the devil out of people:

- When the "angel of the LORD" (thought by many to be an Old Testament appearance of Jesus) burned an offering made by Gideon, the future judge of Israel cried out in fear, believing he would die.
- When the angel Gabriel visited Zechariah in the temple to predict the birth of John the Baptist, the old priest "was startled and was gripped with fear."
- When an angel materialized in the fields near Bethlehem to announce the birth of Jesus, shepherds there saw the "glory of the Lord" and were terrified.
- When a gleaming white angel dropped from heaven to Jesus' empty tomb, rolling the stone away to prove the Lord had risen, the men "protecting" the site fainted away: "The guards were so afraid of him that they shook and became like dead men."

Here's a somewhat more realistic rendition of an angel—powerful in battle, and kicking Satan's tail. This image of the archangel Michael is by the seventeenth-century Italian artist Guido Reni.

YES, SIR!

While angels didn't *always* create fright, they inevitably generated respect:

- When an angel told a dreaming Joseph to take Mary and the baby Jesus to Egypt for safety, the tired carpenter obeyed—leaving "during the night."
- When an angel instructed Philip to take a certain road out of Jerusalem, the evangelist obeyed—and actually *ran* to talk with an Ethiopian eunuch who needed to hear the Gospel.
- When an angel ordered Cornelius to call for Peter, the Roman centurion obeyed—and helped to confirm the great apostle's understanding that God's message was for Gentiles as well as for Jews.

THE WRONG RESPONSE

Considering the fear and deference angels generated, it's hard to imagine anyone disrespecting them. But one Bible character was rebuked for showing *too much* respect to an angel.

You'll find the story in the very last chapter of the Bible, Revelation 22. The apostle John, after receiving an amazing vision of the end times from an angel of God, was so overwhelmed that he dropped to his guide's feet to worship.

"Don't do that!" the angel shouted. "I am a fellow servant with you and with your fellow prophets and with all who keep the words of this scroll. Worship God!"

Not the reaction of some soft, effeminate, chubby kid with wings, huh?

President Abraham Lincoln once had the same experience as the angel of Revelation—and gave the same response—shortly after the fall of Richmond, Virginia, in the American Civil War. Touring the former Confederate capital, Lincoln was surrounded by slaves who cheered his efforts at emancipation. But when one dropped to the president's feet in reverence, Lincoln replied, "You must kneel to God only and thank Him for your freedom."

ANGELIC APPEARANCES TO PEOPLE IN THE BIBLE

- To Hagar, in the wilderness (Genesis 16:7)
- To Abraham (Genesis 18:2, 22:11–18)
- To Lot, in Sodom (Genesis 19:1–17)
- To Jacob, in his various visions (Genesis 28:12)
- To Jacob as he prepared to meet Esau (Genesis 32:1)
- To Moses, in the burning bush (Exodus 3:2)
- To the Israelites (Exodus 14:19; Judges 2:1–4)
- To Balaam (Numbers 22:31)
- To Gideon (Judges 6:11–22)
- To Manoah (Judges 13:6, 15–20)
- To David, at the threshing floor of Araunah (2 Samuel 24:16–27)
- To Elijah, while he lay under the juniper tree (1 Kings 19:5–11)
- To Shadrach, Meshach, and Abednego in the fiery furnace (Daniel 3:25, 28)
- To Daniel (Daniel 6:22; 8:16; 9:21; 10:5–10, 16, 18; 12:5–7)
- To Zechariah, in a vision (Zechariah 1:9, 2:3, 3:1–2, 4:1)
- To Joseph, in a dream (Matthew 1:20; 2:13, 19)
- To Zacharias the priest (Luke 1:11–20)
- To Mary, concerning the upcoming birth of Jesus (Luke 1:26–38)
- To the shepherds, announcing the Messiah's birth (Luke 2:9–14)
- To Jesus, after His temptation (Matthew 4:11)
- To Jesus, in Gethsemane (Luke 22:43)
- At Christ's tomb (Matthew 28:2–5; Mark 16:5–7; Luke 24:23; John 20:12)
- At the ascension (Acts 1:10–11)
- To the apostles, while in prison (Acts 5:19)
- To Philip (Acts 8:26)
- To Cornelius, in a dream (Acts 10:3, 30–32)
- To Peter, in prison (Acts 12:7–11)
- To Paul, on a ship at sea (Acts 27:23)
- To John, at Patmos (Revelation 1:1; 5:2; 7:11; 10:9; 11:15; 17:7; 19:10; 22:8)

An angel escorts Peter from prison in answer to the prayers of the new Christian church meeting in the house of Mary, mother of John Mark. Unfortunately, the pray-ers seemed to doubt the power of their prayers: when Peter arrived at their door, they didn't believe it was really him! See the whole story in Acts 12.

WATER OF JEALOUSY

SCRIPTURES REFERENCED:
EXODUS 20:14; NUMBERS 5:5–31

God made the seventh of His Ten Commandments quite simple: "You shall not commit adultery." His test of obedience to the commandment was considerably more complex.

YOUR CHEATIN' HEART

Of course, God Himself knew if a woman had been unfaithful to her husband—that's what omniscience is all about. But for a man questioning his wife's fidelity, God laid out a process that's surely one of the Bible's greatest oddities. A specific and detailed procedure was to be followed to see if the woman was true:

- Step 1: Husband takes wife to priest along with a grain offering of barley flour.
- Step 2: Priest makes woman stand in God's presence while he mixes a drink—of holy water and dust from the tabernacle floor.
- Step 3: Priest loosens woman's hair and puts grain offering in her hand while he holds the "bitter water."
- Step 4: Priest puts the woman under oath, warning her of dire consequences if she is found to be an adulteress.
- Step 5: Woman acknowledges oath with the words "So be it."
- Step 6: Priest writes consequences of adultery on a scroll, washes the scroll in the dusty water, and makes the woman drink the water.
- Step 7: Priest takes the grain from the woman's hand, waves it before God, and burns some on the altar. Then he makes the woman swig the water again.

THE VERDICT

If the husband's suspicions were unfounded, the water would have no effect on the wife. (Though the two of them would undoubtedly feel an awkwardness in their relationship in days to come.) If, however, the woman was actually guilty, the tabernacle-dust water would cause her "bitter suffering"—her belly would swell, her thigh would waste away, and she would be cursed by her countrymen.

As with all of God's rules, wouldn't it have been better just to obey?

This modern re-creation of the tabernacle, set in the Israeli desert, hints that the priest would have found plenty of dust to use in God's recipe for "bitter water."

THE TEN COMMANDMENTS

- You shall have no other gods before me.
- You shall not make for yourself an image in the form of anything in heaven above or on the earth beneath or in the waters below. You shall not bow down to them or worship them; for I, the LORD your God, am a jealous God, punishing the children for the sin of the parents to the third and fourth generation of those who hate me, but showing love to a thousand generations of those who love me and keep my commandments.
- You shall not misuse the name of the LORD your God, for the LORD will not hold anyone guiltless who misuses his name.
- Remember the Sabbath day by keeping it holy. Six days you shall labor and do all your work, but the seventh day is a sabbath to the LORD your God. On it you shall not do any work, neither you, nor your son or daughter, nor your male or female servant, nor your animals, nor any foreigner residing in your towns. For in six days the LORD made the heavens and the earth, the sea, and all that is in them, but he rested on the seventh day. Therefore the LORD blessed the Sabbath day and made it holy.
- Honor your father and your mother, so that you may live long in the land the LORD your God is giving you.
- You shall not murder.
- You shall not commit adultery.
- You shall not steal.
- You shall not give false testimony against your neighbor.
- You shall not covet your neighbor's house. You shall not covet your neighbor's wife, or his male or female servant, his ox or donkey, or anything that belongs to your neighbor.

Exodus 20:3–17

WHAT THE GOOD BOOK SAYS ABOUT OBEDIENCE

- It should be motivated by love of God (John 14:15).
- It is more important to obey God than men (Acts 5:29).
- It is the result of a changed heart (1 Peter 1:14).
- It is a necessity to those who desire to follow God (2 Kings 18:6).
- It is a decision believers make (Psalm 119:30).
- Jesus demonstrated it perfectly (John 14:31).
- It must be done without hesitation (Psalm 119:60).
- It is proof that God's Spirit is really within us (1 John 3:24).
- It should be done wholeheartedly (2 Chronicles 31:21).
- It is not a burden to those who love God (1 John 5:3).
- It is key to God's blessing and a long life for yourself and your family (Deuteronomy 4:39–40).
- It blesses those who delight in it (Psalm 112:1).
- It is necessary for those who wish to claim God's promises (Deuteronomy 6:18).
- We who are in Christ are created for it (Ephesians 2:10).
- It is necessary to overcome our enemies (Exodus 23:22).
- It is key to eternal life (John 8:51).
- It is motivated by faith (Hebrews 11:7).
- It is done even when no one is watching (Philippians 2:12).
- It results in a clear conscience (Acts 23:1).
- It comes from the heart (Psalm 119:112; Ezra 7:10).
- It is part of our walk with God (Genesis 6:9).

We train animals to be obedient—to do what we want them to do—as the Bible writer James once said: "When we put bits into the mouths of horses to make them obey us, we can turn the whole animal" (James 3:3). Too bad that humans have such a hard time learning those lessons!

THE ARK FOUND!

SCRIPTURES REFERENCED:

EXODUS 25:10–22; EXODUS 26:31–35; HEBREWS 9:4; EXODUS 16:4, 31; NUMBERS 17; DEUTERONOMY 10:1–2; 1 SAMUEL 4–6; 2 CHRONICLES 5; REVELATION 11:19

Forget Indiana Jones...the "lost ark" has been found!

It's not in a creepy cavern guarded by natives, Nazis, or other assorted nasties. The apostle John has pinpointed its location with an X-marks-the-spot description in the book of Revelation.

THE OTHER ARK

Before we go there, though, a little background: We're not talking about *Noah's* ark, that football field–sized barge that saved a few people and a whole lot of animals from a worldwide deluge. The ark that concerns us is the "ark of the covenant," a gold-plated wooden box about 3 feet 9 inches long and 2 feet 3 inches wide and high, containing some very interesting artifacts:

- a jar of manna—that sweet bread from heaven that God rained down on the Israelite camp during the Exodus;
- Aaron's rod—the wooden stick that budded to prove Aaron was God's chosen priest; and
- the stone tablets of the Ten Commandments—inscribed by the finger of God Himself. (Besides the ACLU, who *wouldn't* want to see that set of chiseled rocks on display somewhere?)

But more important than what was *in* the box was what happened *above* the box. Over a cover of pure gold, between the figures of spread-winged angels on either side, God Himself would actually meet with Moses and "give [him] all my commands for the Israelites." Clearly, this was no ordinary box.

The ark of the covenant sat behind a blue, purple, and scarlet curtain in the Most Holy Place of the Israelites' traveling worship center, the tabernacle. The tabernacle had to be portable because it went with the Israelites on their forty-year meander to the Promised Land. And the ark led the way.

WHAT WE KNOW ABOUT THE ARK OF THE COVENANT

- This special box is distinguished from any other chest or coffer with titles such as the "ark of God" (1 Samuel 3:3), the "ark of the covenant" (Joshua 3:6), or the "ark of the testimony" (Exodus 25:22 KJV).
- It was made of acacia or shittim wood, was a cubit and a half wide and high and two cubits long, and covered completely in the purest gold.
- Its upper lid, also known as the mercy-seat, was surrounded with a rim of gold, and on each of the two sides were two gold rings in which were placed two gold-covered poles by which the ark could be carried (Exodus 25:10–22; 37:1–9).
- There were two cherubim (angel) figures over the ark at each end. Their faces were turned toward each other (Exodus 37:9; Numbers 7:89) and their outstretched wings over the top formed the throne of God. The ark itself served as His footstool (1 Chronicles 28:2).
- The ark was placed in the "holy of holies"—the interior portion of the tabernacle—and positioned so that one end of the carrying poles touched the veil separating the two sections of the tabernacle (1 Kings 8:8).
- Stored in the ark were the Ten Commandments on two stone tables, the "pot of manna," and Aaron's "rod that had budded" (Hebrews 9:4).

LOST AND FOUND

Once in the Promised Land, the people got careless and began to think of the ark as a good-luck charm. One time the Israelites took it into battle (a really dumb idea) and lost the ark to their archenemies, the Philistines. Though that was a major blow to the people of Israel, the Philistines actually got the worst end of the deal—coming down with a mysterious ailment that sounds a lot like hemorrhoids (see "Welcome to Emerod City" on page 204).

Before long, as if they were playing a game of hot potato, the Philistines sent the ark back to Israel where it ultimately took a place of honor in the grand temple built by King Solomon. When the Babylonians overran Jerusalem in 586 BC, the ark apparently disappeared, only to be resurrected in Hollywood fashion in the 1981 film *Raiders of the Lost Ark*.

Which brings us back to our main point—where exactly *is* the ark? Buried in some Middle Eastern cave? Tucked away in one of Saddam Hussein's palaces? Not according to the author of Revelation.

Nearly seven centuries after its last known address, John saw the ark in one of his visions. "Then God's temple in heaven was opened," John wrote, "and within his temple was seen the ark of his covenant."

Indiana Jones missed the boat.

THE ARK OF THE COVENANT IS CAPTURED AND RETURNED

The movements of the Ark of the Covenant

Ebenezer?

Aphek

Shiloh

The Ark is brought to the battle from Shiloh but is captured after the Philistines defeat the Israelites

Lod

The Ark is taken to Kiriath-jearim, where it remains for some 20 years

Bethel

Lower Beth-horon
Upper Beth-horon

Mizpah

Gilgal?

Gezer

Aijalon

Ramah

Jericho

Kiriath-jearim

Ekron

Jebus (Jerusalem)

Ashdod

Beth-shemesh

The idol in the temple of Dagon topples over before the Ark

Gath

The Philistines return the Ark to Israel on a wooden cart drawn by two cows

Bethlehem

Ashkelon

Mediterranean Sea

PHILISTIA

Lachish

Hebron

Dead Sea

Jordan River

Copyright © 2007 by Barbour Publishing, Inc.

N

THE TRAVELING ARK

- Before the Israelites settled in the Promised Land, priests would carry the ark in front of the crowds (Numbers 4:5–6).
- The book of Joshua reports that the priests carried it into the bed of the Jordan River, which separated, allowing everyone to pass over (Joshua 3:15–16).
- The ark was carried in procession around before the Israelites took the city (Joshua 6:4–12).
- After the people of Israel settled in the Promised Land, the ark remained in the tabernacle at Gilgal for a time. It was later moved to Shiloh.
- The ark was sometimes carried into fields of battle in hopes of victory, but the Philistines took the ark (1 Samuel 4:3–11). Seven months later, they returned it because it brought a curse on them (1 Samuel 5:7–8).
- After the ark was returned, it remained at Kiriath-jearim (1 Samuel 7:1–2) until the time of King David. The king wanted to move the ark to Jerusalem, but because it was not moved properly, Uzzah lost his life.
- The ark remained in the house of Obed-edom in Gath-rimmon for three months (2 Samuel 6:1–11). David then moved it to Jerusalem, where it remained until a place was prepared for it. Solomon, David's son and successor, later placed the ark in the temple he built (1 Kings 8:6–9).
- But when the Babylonians sacked Jerusalem, the ark disappeared, never to be seen again.

THE HANKY THAT HEALED

SCRIPTURES REFERENCED:
ACTS 19:11–12; LUKE 8:43–48; ACTS 5:12–16; ISAIAH 53:5

When you stop to think about it, handkerchiefs are pretty gross. But in the days before Kleenex, they were also pretty important for dealing with, shall we say, *nasal congestion.*

Of course, handkerchiefs only clear away the *results* of nasal congestion—they don't cure it. Unless, that is, the apostle Paul is involved.

MEN OF THE CLOTH

Early in his third missionary journey, Paul made a stop in Ephesus, an Aegean Sea port in what is now Turkey. Besides sharing the good news of Jesus (for three months in the local synagogue, and two years in the school of a man named Tyrannus), Paul performed many "extraordinary miracles" in the city. These sometimes involved his touching handkerchiefs, which were then delivered to people in need, curing their sicknesses and driving out their demons. The process worked with aprons, too.

Though that might seem a bit strange, there was precedent for a bit of cloth transferring healing power. Once, near Jesus' headquarters of Capernaum, a woman who suffered from bleeding approached the Lord. She'd had the problem for twelve long years and "had spent all her living upon physicians" (KJV). But with a quick stroke of the edge of Jesus' cloak, the bleeding stopped.

The apostle Paul is often shown in classic art holding a sword, perhaps a reference to the tradition that says he was beheaded with a sword, or perhaps a symbol of his description of God's Word as "the sword of the Spirit" (Ephesians 6:17). This painting is by the sixteenth- and seventeenth-century master El Greco.

PAUL THE MIRACLE-WORKING APOSTLE

As Jesus promised they would, the apostles performed many miracles—including healings and raising the dead—that pointed people toward the truth of their message. While Paul was not among the original Twelve, he also performed miracles by the power of God.

Paul wrote to the Roman Christians, "I will not venture to speak of anything except what Christ has accomplished through me in leading the Gentiles to obey God by what I have said and done—by the power of signs and wonders, through the power of the Spirit of God" (Romans 15:18–19). And to the church at Corinth, he wrote, "I persevered in demonstrating among you the marks of a true apostle, including signs, wonders and miracles" (2 Corinthians 12:12).

While Paul made reference in his letters to the miracles he had performed, he didn't spell out for his readers what they were. But Luke the physician, who wrote the accounts of Paul's ministry in the book of Acts, reported several instances of Paul's miracle-working:

- Paul blinds Elymas, a false prophet/sorcerer who was attempting to keep them from preaching the Gospel (Acts 13:6–11).
- Paul heals a lame man in Lystra (Acts 14:8–10).
- Paul performs many miracles, including healings and the casting out of demons (Acts 19:11–12).
- Paul raises Eutychus, a young man who had fallen out of an upstairs window, from the dead (Acts 20:9–12).
- Paul heals diseases in Malta (Acts 28:8–9).

A photo of "Saint Paul's Bay" in Malta, where tradition says the apostle was shipwrecked. In that case, Paul was on the receiving end of miracles: An angel told Paul of the coming disaster, but assured him that all 276 people on the ship would be saved—then later, on shore, Paul was bitten by a poisonous snake while collecting firewood. He simply shook the snake into the fire, and continued with his work (see Acts 27–28).

CREDIT WHERE CREDIT IS DUE

It wasn't a magical cloth that healed those people; it was a miracle-working God—who could use even the shadow of the apostle Peter to accomplish His medical purposes: "People brought the sick into the streets and laid them on beds and mats so that at least Peter's shadow might fall on some of them as he passed by."

Those physical healings were very cool but were only temporary. Of far greater impact is the spiritual healing God gives through Jesus: "He was pierced for our transgressions, he was crushed for our iniquities; the punishment that brought us peace was on him, and by his wounds we are healed."

ISAIAH'S PROPHECIES OF THE MESSIAH, JESUS CHRIST

Prophecy	Reference	Fulfillment
Born of a virgin	Isaiah 7:14	Matthew 1:18
Sent by God	Isaiah 48:16	John 7:29
A light to the Gentiles	Isaiah 9:1–2	Luke 2:28–32
Came to glorify God	Isaiah 49:3	Matthew 15:30–31
Preached the good news	Isaiah 61:1–2	Luke 4:17–22
Spoke in parables	Isaiah 6:9–10	Matthew 13:13–15
Ministered in Galilee	Isaiah 9:1–2	Matthew 4:12–17
Had compassion for the poor	Isaiah 42:3	Matthew 11:4–5
Healed the blind	Isaiah 35:5	Mark 10:51–52
Healed the deaf	Isaiah 35:5	Mark 7:32–35
Healed the lame	Isaiah 35:6	Matthew 12:10–13
Rejected by His own people	Isaiah 53:3	John 1:11
Grieved over the Jews' unbelief	Isaiah 49:4	Luke 19:41–42
Suffered willingly	Isaiah 53:11	John 12:27
Gave up His life to save humankind	Isaiah 53:12	Luke 23:46
Shed His blood for all	Isaiah 52:15	Revelation 1:5
Oppressed and afflicted	Isaiah 53:7	Matthew 27:27–31
Silent when accused	Isaiah 53:7	Matthew 26:62–63
Suffered for others	Isaiah 53:4–5	Matthew 8:16–17
His face beaten and spat upon	Isaiah 50:6	Matthew 26:67
His back whipped	Isaiah 50:6	Matthew 27:26
Crucified with sinners	Isaiah 53:12	Matthew 27:38

BIBLE DIET PLANS

SCRIPTURES REFERENCED:
DANIEL 1; MATTHEW 3:1–6; EZEKIEL 2–3

Weight Watchers, Atkins, Sugar Busters, South Beach—there are almost as many diet plans as there are dieters. Each carries an implied promise of better health, more energy, and drop-dead-gorgeous good looks to those who follow the prescribed list of dietary dos and don'ts.

But that's nothing new—though their motives differed, even Bible characters had special diets.

VEGGIE TALES

Have you heard about the Daniel in Babylon Diet Plan? Yes, *that* Daniel—of Daniel and the lions' den fame. He was one of the princely young men of Israel carried off to conquering Babylon (the area of modern-day Iraq) about six hundred years before Christ. The Babylonian king, Nebuchadnezzar, planned to train these upstanding young men to serve in his palace. The training included chow—some of Nebuchadnezzar's finest foods and wines.

As a believer in the one true God, Daniel didn't want to "defile" himself by eating the pagan king's choice foods, so he asked instead for a menu of water and vegetables (*pulse* in the King James Version). Also trying the Daniel in Babylon Diet Plan were three guys named Hananiah, Mishael, and Azariah. You might know them better as Shadrach, Meshach, and Abednego.

The Babylonian overseeing the Israelites, a man named Ashpenaz, wasn't so sure about Daniel's idea: "I am afraid of my lord the king, who has assigned your food and drink. Why should he see you looking worse than the other young men your age? The king would then have my head because of you."

But Daniel knew he was on to something good. "Please test your servants for ten days," he suggested to his guard. "Then compare our appearance with that of the young men who eat the royal food." The guard agreed, and a week and a half later, the four friends were looking healthier and better nourished than all the other guys eating the king's fancy fare. In no time, *everyone* was on the Daniel in Babylon Diet Plan—whether they wanted to be or not: "So the guard took away their choice food and the wine they were to drink and gave them vegetables instead."

NEW NAMES. . .

There are several examples in the Bible of people whose names changed when their purpose in life changed—Abram became Abraham, Sarai became Sarah, Saul became Paul, just to name a few. The first chapter of the book of Daniel includes the account of four men, including Daniel himself, who received new names:

- **Daniel to Belteshazzar (Daniel 1:6–7)**
  The Hebrew prophet Daniel received the Babylonian name Belteshazzar when he entered King Nebuchadnezzar's service.
- **Hananiah to Shadrach (Daniel 1:6–7)**
  Hananiah, one of Daniel's friends, received the Babylonian name Shadrach at the same time Daniel received the name Belteshazzar. The name Hananiah means "God has favored."
- **Mishael to Meshach (Daniel 1:6–7)**
  A friend and companion of the prophet Daniel who received the Babylonian name Meshach. The Hebrew name Mishael means "Who is what God is?"
- **Azariah to Abed-nego (Daniel 1:6–7)**
  The Babylonian name for Azariah, the third of Daniel's companions in exile. The Hebrew name Azariah means "God has helped."

UNUSUAL DISHES

If you think an all-vegetable diet plan would be boring, at least it offers more variety than the John the Baptist Diet Plan. Developed by the man who "prepared the way" for Jesus Christ, the JB Diet came out of the Judean desert and allowed only two foods: wild honey (sounds okay) and locusts (ewwww).

And then there was the Ezekiel Diet, guaranteed to change your life. This unusual eating plan came to the prophet in a vision from God: "Then I looked, and I saw a hand stretched out to me. In it was a scroll, which he unrolled before me. On both sides of it were written words of lament and mourning and woe. And he said to me, 'Son of man, eat what is before you, eat this scroll.'"

Ezekiel reports that the scroll was like sweet honey going down, though its words of judgment came back bitterly to the Jewish exiles in Babylon. The scroll apparently provided Ezekiel at least twenty-five years' worth of energy for prophesying.

Girl with a Pomegranate by William-Adolphe Bouguereau (1875).

YUM! FOODS MENTIONED IN THE BIBLE

Apples	Leeks
Almonds	Lentils
Barley	Locust
Bread	Melons
Beans	Milk
Butter	Olives
Calf	Olive Oil
Cheese	Onions
Corn	Partridge
Cucumbers	Pigeon
Dates	Pistachio Nuts
Dove	Pomegranates
Eggs	Quail
Figs	Raisins
Fish	Sheep
Flour	Sycamore Fruit
Goat	Unleavened Bread
Grapes	Venison
Grape Juice	Vinegar
Honey	Wheat
Lamb	Wine

GOVERNMENT RUNS AMOK

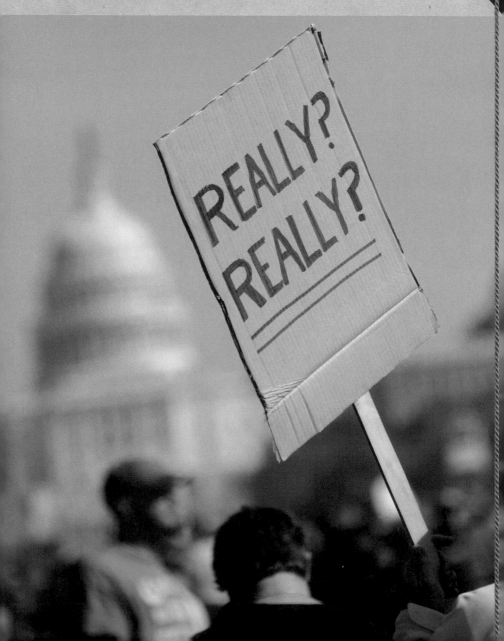

SCRIPTURES REFERENCED:

1 KINGS 16:29–33; 1 KINGS 21–22; EXODUS 22:28; LEVITICUS 24:10–16;
DEUTERONOMY 17:6; ROMANS 13:1–5

Those of us who fret over the intrusiveness of modern government can be thankful we didn't live in the kingdom of Ahab.

Ahab ruled around about nine hundred years before Jesus. He is considered the rottenest apple in a long line of bad kings of the northern kingdom of Israel, the ten tribes that split from the clans of Benjamin and Judah after the death of Solomon. According to the Bible's first book of Kings, Ahab "did more evil in the eyes of the LORD than any of those before him."

BUT WAIT—THERE'S MORE

Though Ahab was awful, he had an even worse wife—Jezebel—whose name in our modern vocabulary describes a bold, shameless woman. An idol worshipper from the seacoast city of Sidon, Jezebel led Ahab away from the one true God and into the worship of Baal. And she masterminded one of history's most egregious examples of governmental overreach.

It happened this way: Ahab wanted to plant a vegetable garden, and he found some land in the town of Jezreel, not far from his palace in Samaria, that was just perfect. Well, *almost* perfect. The plot, a vineyard, was owned by a man named

Jezebel's god—Baal—holds a lightning bolt in this stele dating to about 1400 BC. Unfortunately for Jezebel, Baal wasn't much help when the one true God decreed her death.

Naboth, who didn't care to part with it, not even for Ahab's offer of a better vineyard in trade or payment for the land's true value.

Stymied, Ahab went home and sulked. When Jezebel found Ahab on his bed, refusing to eat, she asked what was eating *him*, and when she found out, she put a simple but lethal plan into action to get Ahab his garden.

On the king's letterhead, Jezebel ordered the leaders of Jezreel to proclaim a day of fasting and to seat Naboth in a place of prominence at a gathering of townspeople. If you're thinking "setup" at this point, you're absolutely right.

Jezebel's next instruction was to put "two scoundrels opposite him and have them bring charges that he has cursed both God and the king." Though she was a Baal worshipper, Jezebel understood God's law well enough to know that cursing God and the king were specifically forbidden—and that at least one of them could lead to the death penalty.

Unfortunately for Naboth, that's exactly what he got. Falsely accused by two "witnesses" (the law required at least two to convict a person of a capital crime), Naboth was taken outside the city and stoned to death. The dirty deed accomplished, Jezebel, bossy as ever, ordered Ahab to go get his garden.

Naboth's government failed him terribly, but after sowing the wind, it would soon reap the whirlwind.

Jezebel's demise, as illustrated by Gustave Doré and stated by the Bible: "Then Jehu went to Jezreel. When Jezebel heard about it, she put on eye makeup, arranged her hair and looked out of a window. As Jehu entered the gate, she asked, 'Have you come in peace, you Zimri, you murderer of your master?' He looked up at the window and called out, 'Who is on my side? Who?' Two or three eunuchs looked down at him. 'Throw her down!' Jehu said. So they threw her down, and some of her blood spattered the wall and the horses as they trampled her underfoot. Jehu went in and ate and drank. 'Take care of that cursed woman,' he said, 'and bury her, for she was a king's daughter.' But when they went out to bury her, they found nothing except her skull, her feet and her hands. They went back and told Jehu, who said, 'This is the word of the LORD that he spoke through his servant Elijah the Tishbite: On the plot of ground at Jezreel dogs will devour Jezebel's flesh. Jezebel's body will be like dung on the ground in the plot at Jezreel, so that no one will be able to say, "This is Jezebel"' (2 Kings 9:30–37).

JUSTICE, OLD TESTAMENT—STYLE

The prophet Elijah found Ahab in Naboth's vineyard and shared God's take on the whole sleazy story: "This is what the LORD says: Have you not murdered a man and seized his property?" Ahab, of course, already knew that. What he didn't know was the punishment God had planned—which fell from Elijah's lips like a bomb: "In the place where dogs licked up Naboth's blood, dogs will lick up your blood—yes, yours!" Justice would pursue Ahab's wife, Jezebel, in a similar fashion: "Dogs will devour Jezebel by the wall of Jezreel."

While modern-day courts sometimes allow the guilty to go unpunished, God's judgment on Ahab and Jezebel was not to be denied. The king got his due in battle at a town called Ramoth Gilead. Assuming correctly that the enemy forces would be gunning for him as king, Ahab disguised himself to fight as a common soldier. The ruse worked—until God stepped in. At that point, "someone drew his bow at random and hit the king of Israel between the sections of his armor." Ahab died slowly, bleeding until death came in the evening.

But didn't God say something about dogs licking up Ahab's blood? Oh, yes—that happened when Ahab's chariot was brought back to Samaria. Townspeople washed it by a pool the prostitutes used for bathing, "and the dogs licked up his blood, as the word of the LORD had declared." Then God fixed his crosshairs on Jezebel, and she died a miserable death at her appointed time (see "What a Way to Go" on page 100). Naboth was avenged, his overreaching government brought to the ultimate judgment.

Too bad Ahab and Jezebel couldn't have led their country the way God wanted them to, the way the apostle Paul wrote in Romans: "Do you want to be free from fear of the one in authority? Then do what is right and you will be commended. For the one in authority is God's servant for your good." Too bad they missed that basic lesson in Government 101.

THERE *IS* SUCH A THING AS A FREE LUNCH

SCRIPTURES REFERENCED:
MATTHEW 14:13—21; MARK 6:30—44; LUKE 9:10—17; JOHN 6:1—15; 10:22—38; 14:1—6

Maybe it's our love of eating that makes the story of Jesus feeding the five thousand so popular. The account is a staple of kids' Sunday school classes, and, like the art of riding a bike, it's something a person never forgets.

Sure, you know the story: A large crowd of people is following Jesus, and late in the day He tells His disciples to feed them. They come up with five small loaves of bread and two fish, and Jesus miraculously parlays that single lunch into a feast for a throng.

An Israeli boat captain casts a net on the Sea of Galilee, setting for Jesus' feeding of the 5,000. At least four of Jesus' disciples—sets of brothers Peter and Andrew, James and John—were fishermen by trade, using techniques similar to that shown here.

DETAILS, DETAILS

We could stop with the outline and say, "That's nice." But the details, mixed together from accounts in each of the four Gospels, enrich the story like vitamins in cereal. Let's pour out a bowlful and pore over the miracle.

The Gospel of John notes that the time was close to the Passover. Since the next time the Passover is mentioned Jesus is being arrested and crucified, we can surmise that the miracle happened one year before His death.

Another death was more immediate. Jesus' relative and forerunner, John the Baptist, had just been beheaded by the Judean ruler Herod Antipas. When that grisly news arrived, Jesus called His disciples to "get some rest" for a while, and they all climbed into a boat on the Sea of Galilee.

Today, the disciples could buy fish sandwiches at an Israeli McDonalds—though an order for 5,000 would necessitate some advance notice and a pretty good chunk of cash. In Jesus' day, a young boy's simple lunch of bread and fish was more than enough to satisfy thousands.

Landing on the north shore of the big lake at a town called Bethsaida, Jesus and company found not a place of quiet reflection but rather a huge crowd of people who had seen the Lord's earlier miracles, learned of His route, and followed Him there. The change of plans was no problem to Jesus, though—all of the Gospel writers note that the Lord simply adjusted His agenda to accommodate the people:

- Luke: "He welcomed them and spoke to them about the kingdom of God, and healed those who needed healing."
- Matthew: "He had compassion on them and healed their sick."
- Mark: "He had compassion on them, because they were like sheep without a shepherd. So he began teaching them many things."

CHOW TIME

John observes that Jesus promptly planned for the crowd's physical needs. "Where shall we buy bread for these people to eat?" Jesus asked His disciple Philip. Though the sentence was phrased in the form of a question, John's Gospel says it wasn't really an interrogative: "He asked this only to test him, for he already had in mind what he was going to do."

As the day wore on, other disciples began to worry about the huge mass of people growing hungrier and more tired—and, perhaps, a little cranky. "Send the people away," they urged Jesus, "so that they can go to the surrounding countryside and villages and buy themselves something to eat."

Jesus' response was simple—and simply crazy: "You give them something to eat."

Philip had performed some mental calculations on Jesus' earlier question, determining that it would require eight months' wages to buy enough food for the crowd—and even that would give each person only a nibble.

When Jesus suggested that the disciples find out how much food was already on hand, Peter's brother spoke up. "Here is a boy with five small barley loaves and two small fish," Andrew said, "but how far will they go among so many?"

HOW FAR, INDEED

That's an odd question for a group of men who had seen Jesus heal the sick, cast out demons, and even talk a wild storm into submission. But Jesus didn't scold them for a lack of faith—He just prepared to dazzle them once again with a display of His power.

While the disciples told the crowd to sit down in the grass, dividing the people into groups of fifties and hundreds, Jesus took the few loaves and fishes and offered a prayer of thanks. (If you've ever wondered why people pray before meals, this might be your answer.)

PHYSICAL POSTURES FOR PRAYER IN THE BIBLE

- Bowing heads: "And they believed. And when they heard that the LORD was concerned about them and had seen their misery, they bowed down and worshiped" (Exodus 4:31).

- Standing: "Then Solomon stood before the altar of the LORD in front of the whole assembly of Israel, spread out his hands toward heaven" (1 Kings 8:22).

- Kneeling: "When Solomon had finished all these prayers and supplications to the LORD, he rose from before the altar of the LORD, where he had been kneeling with his hands spread out toward heaven" (1 Kings 8:54).

- On their faces before God: "Jehoshaphat bowed down with his face to the ground, and all the people of Judah and Jerusalem fell down in worship before the LORD" (2 Chronicles 20:18; also see Matthew 26:39).

Orthodox Jews pray at Jerusalem's Western Wall. One of the most sacred sites of Judaism, the wall is what's left of the former Jewish temple.

Then Jesus began tearing the loaves apart, handing out pieces to His disciples to hand out to the crowd. Jesus did the same with the fish, and just kept tearing and handing, tearing and handing, tearing and handing until the five thousand men in the crowd had had enough to fill their stomachs. Forget that little nibble Philip had suggested.

The crowd was probably much larger than five thousand, though, because Matthew notes that the number doesn't include women and children—and if you figure many of the men had wives, and many of the couples had kids with them, the number fed could swell to ten or fifteen thousand.

Not only were thousands of people fed to fullness, but the disciples were able to pick up twelve baskets of leftovers—"Let nothing be wasted," Jesus said. And so, each one of the Lord's helpers knew where his next several meals would come from.

A fifteen-hundred-year-old mosaic commemorates Jesus' miracle at the Church of the Multiplication of the Loaves and Fishes in Tabgha, Israel, on the northwest shore of the Sea of Galilee.

THE REASON WHY

The Bible doesn't say how long it took Jesus to break the bread and fish, or how much time the disciples needed to distribute the food to the small groups sitting in the grass. But it must have been a relatively slow process, allowing both the crowd and the disciples to marvel at what was happening.

Marveling is fine, but the crowd quickly came to the wrong conclusion about Jesus, who slipped away privately before they could try to "make him king by force." As people often do, they missed the point of Jesus' miracle.

Why would He feed thousands of people with one little boy's lunch? To direct those people to the Father: "Do not believe me unless I do the works of my Father," Jesus later told a crowd of unbelieving Jews who accused Him of blasphemy. "But if I do them, even though you do not believe me, believe the works, that you may know and understand that the Father is in me, and I in the Father." And even later, talking with His disciples, Jesus said, "I am the way and the truth and the life. No one comes to the Father except through me."

The benefits of Jesus' free lunch lasted a few hours. The benefits of His free gift of salvation—of adoption by God the Father—are eternal.

FOOD-RELATED MIRACLES IN THE BIBLE

- God sends manna for Israelites to eat daily, except on the Sabbath (Exodus 16:14–35)
- God sends quail for the Israelites to eat (Numbers 11:4–6, 31–34)
- Widow of Zarephath's flour and oil increased (1 Kings 17:14–16)
- Elijah fed by ravens (1 Kings 17:2–6)
- The widow's oil multiplied (2 Kings 4:2–7)
- The deadly stew cured with flour at Gilgal (2 Kings 4:38–41)
- A hundred men fed with twenty loaves at Gilgal (2 Kings 4:42–44)
- A miraculous catch of fish (Luke 5:4–11)
- Jesus turns water into wine (John 2:1–11)
- Jesus feeds 5,000 (Matthew 14:13–21; Mark 6:30–44; Luke 9:10–17; John 6:1–13)
- Jesus feeds 4,000 (Matthew 15:32; Mark 8:1)
- Jesus curses a fig tree (Matthew 21:18–19; Mark 11:12–14)

Dinner's on God tonight—the incredible, edible quail

THE FREE LUNCH PREVIEW

SCRIPTURES REFERENCED:
2 KINGS 1–4; HEBREWS 13:8

Let's get one thing clear from the start: We're not saying that God would ever need to "practice" anything He does. But tucked into the book of 2 Kings is a kind of "trial run" of Jesus' feeding of the five thousand. Ever heard about this small marvel?

THE FEEDING OF THE ONE HUNDRED

A Russian icon of the early eighteenth century shows Elisha with a prominent forehead. Some kids learned the hard way that they shouldn't make fun of baldness (see 2 Kings 2:23–25).

The prophet Elisha is the central character in this little drama. Not long after Elijah hitched a ride to heaven (see "Men Escape Death—Permanently" on page 124), Elisha performed a string of miracles to establish his credentials with the people of Israel: he divided the Jordan River with Elijah's cloak, healed a poison spring with a dash of salt, called bears from the hills to maul some punk kids who were jeering at his baldness, kept a widow's oil supply flowing during a famine, and even raised

THE LIFE OF THE PROPHET ELISHA

- Elisha was from Abel Meholah (1 Kings 19:16), a city in the Jordan River valley, halfway between the Sea of Galilee and the Dead Sea.
- He was the son of a farmer named Shaphat (1 Kings 19:19).
- Elisha was plowing his father's fields when Elijah found him and called him to follow (1 Kings 19:19).
- The name Elisha means "God is salvation."
- Elisha was successor to the prophet Elijah and received a "double portion" of Elijah's spirit (2 Kings 2:9).
- Elisha ministered as a prophet in Israel from about 850–800 BC, during the reigns of the Israelite kings Joram, Jehu, Jehoahaz, and Joash.
- Accounts of Elisha's life and ministry are found in 1 and 2 Kings.
- Elisha called the leadership of Israel to turn back to the Lord and to acknowledge God's sovereignty over every aspect of life.
- Though Elijah was constantly in conflict with the political authorities in Israel, Elisha had a more cordial relationship with them.
- Elisha performed many miracles— he healed a polluted water source for the people of Jericho, provided oil for a widow, and caused a "great woman" of Shunem to have a child then brought him back to life after he died. He fed a hundred people from twenty loaves of bread.
- At Elisha's command, Naaman, captain of the Syrian king, bathed in the Jordan and was healed of leprosy.

the woman's dead son back to life. (Want additional details? See "Miracle Man 2" on page 16.)

God had a "company of prophets" about a hundred strong. Elisha assumed the leadership Elijah had once had, in part by appealing to the men's hearts through their stomachs. First, Elisha healed a pot of poison stew made from wild vines. (A pinch of flour did the trick.) Then he foreshadowed Jesus' miraculous feeding of thousands by multiplying twenty new loaves of bread into a meal for all hundred guys.

"How can I set this before a hundred men?" his skeptical servant asked. But Elisha pressed on: "Give it to the people to eat. For this is what the LORD says: 'They will eat and have some left over.'"

WORTH REPEATING

Some nine hundred years later, though on a much larger scale, Jesus would follow the very same pattern. That's not surprising, considering that He's "the same yesterday and today and forever."

15 MIRACLES ASSOCIATED WITH ELISHA

- Parting of the Jordan (2 Kings 2:14)
- Healing of the water (2 Kings 2:21)
- Curse of the bears (2 Kings 2:24)
- Filling of the valley with water (2 Kings 3:17)
- Deception of the Moabites (2 Kings 3:22)
- Miracle of the vessels of oil (2 Kings 4:4)
- Resurrection of the Shunammite's son (2 Kings 4:34)
- Healing of the stew with flour (2 Kings 4:41)
- Feeding one hundred men with twenty loaves of barley bread (2 Kings 4:43)
- Healing of Naaman (2 Kings 5:14)
- Cursing Gehazi with leprosy (2 Kings 5:26–27)
- The floating iron ax head (2 Kings 6:6)
- Striking the Syrian army with blindness and then restoring their sight (2 Kings 6:18–20)
- Deception of the Syrians with the sound of chariots (2 Kings 7:6)
- Resurrection of the man touched by his bones (2 Kings 13:21)

A woman of Shunem sees her son raised back to life by the prophet Elisha. The well-to-do woman had previously provided lodging for Elisha whenever he was traveling through. As a thank-you, Elisha had passed along God's blessed news: that she would conceive and bear a son within the year. When the boy later suffered a piercing headache and died, Elisha performed yet another miracle, bringing him back to life (see 2 Kings 4). By the way, this story contains the Bible's only reference to sneezing.

THE PROPHETS OF
ISRAEL AND JUDAH

Prophet Prophet's birthplace or
primary area of ministry

Mediterranean Sea

ARAM

Dan

Hazor

Jonah
Gath-hepher

Sea of Galilee

Aphek?

Mount Carmel

Kishon River

Megiddo

Jezreel

Lo-debar?

Beth-arbel

I S R A E L

Abel-meholah

Elijah
Tishbe?

Elisha

Samaria

G I L E A D

Ahijah   *Jehu Hosea*

Gilgal?   Shiloh

Joppa

Jordan River

*Isaiah
Zephaniah
Haggai
Zechariah
Malachi*
Bethel

Jeremiah

Nahum

Jericho
Elkosh

Anathoth

Jerusalem

P H I L I S T I A

Micah

J U D A H

Moresheth-gath?

Tekoa

Amos

Dead Sea

0 5 10   20   30 mi
0 10 20 30 40 km

Copyright © 2007 by Barbour Publishing, Inc.

N

THE OTHER NOAH

SCRIPTURES REFERENCED:
NUMBERS 26:29–33; NUMBERS 27:1–11; NUMBERS 36:1–13; JOSHUA 17:1–6

Everybody knows Noah, the guy with the floating zoo. But what about the Bible's other Noah?

There are *two* Noahs in the pages of scripture, and the second one's a she. Perhaps her father, Zelophehad, named her after the hero of the great flood. And though this female Noah carried a man's name, at least she wasn't saddled with her sister's moniker: Hoglah.

A QUESTION OF INHERITANCE

Noah and Hoglah were among five daughters born to Zelophehad. Mr. Z., a descendant of Jacob by way of Joseph by way of Manasseh by way of Gilead, never had a son. And in Bible times, sons got most of the goodies— including the inheritance of land when Daddy died.

Well, Zelophehad did die, as one of the Israelites wandering the wilderness. His five girls, looking ahead to the partition of the Promised Land, went to Moses with a question: "Why should our father's name disappear from his clan because he had no son? Give us property among our father's relatives."

Moses took the issue directly to God, who agreed with the five women—and set up a rule going forward that the property of any son-less man who died should go first to his daughters, if he had any. . .if not, to his brothers. . .if none of them, to his uncles. . .and if none of them, to the closest relative available.

We have no record of Zelophehad leaving a will—though, at the time, the question was moot because he had no sons. It took his daughters' boldness to gain God's formal ruling that the daughters of son-less men could inherit property when daddy passed on.

ONE STIPULATION

The boldness of Noah and her sisters got them the land they wanted, but it also limited their potential marriage partners. Leaders of the Gilead families suggested to Moses that when Zelophehad's girls got married, they might marry into different tribes of Israel—and that their land would then become part of their husbands' tribes. Once again, Moses took the issue to God, who made a ruling: The five women could only marry within their father's clan. And they did, marrying cousins on their father's side.

The daughters of Zelophehad had the strength of sisterhood on their side. But more importantly, they had God on their side.

UNISEX NAMES OF THE BIBLE

Abiah (2 men, 1 woman)

Abihail (3 men, 2 women)

Abijah (5 men, 1 woman)

Ahlai (1 man, 1 woman)

Aholibamah (1 man, 1 woman)

Anah (2 men, 1 woman)

Athaliah (2 men, 1 woman)

Ephah (2 men, 1 woman)

Gomer (1 man, 1 woman)

Hushim (2 men, 1 woman)

Joanna (1 man, 1 woman)

Maacah (1 men, 1 woman)

Maachah (4 men, 6 women)

Michaiah (4 men, 1 woman)

Noadiah (1 man, 1 woman)

Noah (1 man, 1 woman)

Puah (2 men, 1 woman)

Shelomith (5 men, 2 women)

Timna (1 man, 2 women)

EIGHTEEN MOST COMMON WOMEN'S NAMES IN THE BIBLE

Mary (7 women)

Maachah (6)

Tamar (3)

Abigail (2)

Abihail (2)

Adah (2)

Ahinoam (2)

Azubah (2)

Bashemath (2)

Deborah (2)

Mahalath (2)

Milcah (2)

Miriam (2)

Naamah (2)

Sarah (2)

Shelomith (2)

Shua (2)

Timna (2)

A British postage stamp of the 1980s shows one of the Bible's seven Marys—the mother of Jesus. Mary is the most common women's name in scripture, followed by Maachah.

BAD APPLES ON JESUS' FAMILY TREE

SCRIPTURES REFERENCED:

HEBREWS 4:14—15; MATTHEW 1:1—17; LUKE 3:23—38; JOSHUA 2; GENESIS 38; 2 KINGS 21; 2 CHRONICLES 33; 2 SAMUEL 11; MATTHEW 9:12

Some people joke about "thieves and cattle rustlers" in their family trees. Even Jesus could join in that conversation.

He, of course, was perfect. The Bible's book of Hebrews calls Jesus our "high priest," who was "tempted in every way, just as we are—yet he did not sin." But, oh, the line from which He came.

THE GOOD, THE BAD, AND THE UGLY

You'll find Jesus' genealogy in two of the four Gospels—in lists of often obscure, hard-to-pronounce names that trace the Son of God's human bloodline all the way back to Abraham in Matthew's account. Luke's Gospel takes the roots of the family tree even deeper—all the way back to Adam.

Some real characters populate those genealogies. Characters like idol worshippers, a murderer, prostitutes, and a man who consorted with prostitutes—at times, it's a motley crew.

Matthew's genealogy, for example, mentions a Rahab in Jesus' line. She's identified as the mother of Boaz, who was the great-grandfather of King

As with the ancient Jews, today's Church of Jesus Christ of Latter-Day Saints (popularly known as the Mormons) puts great emphasis on genealogy and family history. This is the church's "Family History Library" in Salt Lake City, Utah, used even by many non-Mormons to trace their own family histories.

David. And it's very possible that she was the prostitute who protected Joshua's spies in the Promised Land. Like a Hollywood harlot-with-a-heart-of-gold, Rahab seemed to atone for her vocation by that act of kindness to the Israelite soldiers—so much so that she earned a spot in the Faith Hall of Fame in Hebrews 11.

HYPOCRITE EXPOSED

It's the Hall of *Shame* for others in Jesus' family tree, though. Take, for example, Judah, who mistook his own daughter-in-law for a prostitute. A son of Jacob, Judah headed up one of the twelve tribes of Israel. When it came time to find a wife for his oldest son, Er ("What do I wanna name 'im? I dunno. *Er*. . ."), Judah found a gal named Tamar. But Er was such a rotten egg that God actually killed him. Son number two, Onan, was expected to fulfill his older brother's husbandly duties to Tamar, but he refused—and got the divine ax, as well.

In baseball terms, it was two-up, two-down for Judah's boys—and Dad was afraid his third son, Shelah, might make the third out to end the inning. Trouble was, Judah had already told Tamar to wait around until Shelah reached marrying age. When Shelah reached that age and Judah "forgot" to set up a wedding, Tamar took matters into her own hands, disguising herself as a prostitute on a road she knew Judah would travel.

The old man took the bait, asking the veiled Tamar to sleep with him in exchange for a young goat from his flock. As promise of payment, he gave the "prostitute" his staff and his seal, with a cord attached. But before Judah could deliver the goat, Tamar disappeared.

In a nineteenth-century painting by Horace Vernet, Judah approaches his own daughter-in-law, Tamar, who has disguised herself as a prostitute. Bad things are bound to happen.

THE LIFE OF JUDAH

- Judah was one of the twelve sons of Jacob/Israel.
- The name Judah means "to praise."
- Judah's mother was Leah, one of Jacob's two wives (the other was Rachel), who also gave birth to Reuben, Levi, Simeon, Issachar and Zebulun.
- Judah was the founder of one of the twelve tribes of Israel. The region of Israel that included the city of Jerusalem was named after Judah.
- The southern kingdom that came into existence after Israel divided into two kingdoms ago was called Judah.
- In the book of Genesis, Judah emerges as a leader in his family.
- Judah was instrumental in saving the life of his brother Joseph, whose brothers plotted to throw Joseph in a pit and leave him to die. Judah persuaded his brothers to instead sell Joseph to a passing group of Ishmaelites (see Genesis 37:26–28).
- The Gospel of Matthew traces the ancestry of Joseph, the earthly father of Jesus, back to Judah.
- In Jacob's blessing of his twelve sons, in Genesis 49, he called Judah a "lion cub" and said that he would have his hand on the necks of his enemies and that his brothers would praise him.

The "Lion of Judah" is a key feature of the city of Jerusalem's emblem. The patriarch Jacob (who God renamed "Israel") called his fourth-born son a "lion's cub" in a deathbed blessing (Genesis 49:8–12).

Later, when townspeople found that Tamar was pregnant, Judah indignantly denounced her, ordering that she be burned to death. At that point, Tamar calmly produced Judah's staff, seal, and cord, saying, "I am pregnant by the man who owns these." Rubbing it in a bit, she added, "See if you recognize whose seal and cord and staff these are."

This man appears in the human family line of Jesus Christ?

"Here is a trustworthy saying that deserves full acceptance: Christ Jesus came into the world to save sinners" (the apostle Paul, 1 Timothy 1:15).

SORRY KINGS

Well, how about David? Yes, King David—Israel's greatest ruler, successful military commander, writer of beautiful psalms, and "man after [God's] own heart." It's hard to ignore, however, his adultery with I-saw-her-taking-a-Bath-sheba, and the fact that he then plotted to have her husband, Uriah, killed on the battlefield.

But, wait—as the Ginsu knife commercials used to say—there's more!

Consider Manasseh. He was a king—but that's about the only good thing to say about him. Crowned at age twelve, Manasseh spent most of the next fifty-five years doing "evil in the eyes of the LORD, following the detestable practices of the nations the LORD had driven out before the Israelites." Not only did Manasseh worship false gods himself, but he actually put an idol in the temple—*God's* temple—in Jerusalem. The occult was a favorite pastime of Manasseh, as he "practiced divination and witchcraft, sought omens, and consulted mediums and spiritists." And, most disgusting of all, this king of God's chosen people "sacrificed his children in the fire." *This* man appears in Jesus' human family tree?

YOU, TOO?

In fact, he does. Just like the sincere but flawed David, just like the deceitful, immoral Judah, just like the prostitute Rahab. Just like the loyal and loving Ruth, who came from the idol-worshipping, child-sacrificing nation of Moab.

Jesus' human family tree is actually a picture of all people—with some seriously messed-up dudes, some decent folks with baggage, and everything in between; and every last one of them incapable of pleasing a perfect God. But that's why Jesus came in the first place—to provide the way of salvation.

"It is not the healthy who need a doctor, but the sick," Jesus once said. He found plenty of sickos in His own human family line. He'll find them in ours, too.

A good shepherd "lays down his life for the sheep" (Jesus, John 10:11).

TWENTY-FIVE IMPORTANT NAMES/TITLES OF JESUS:

- Advocate (1 John 2:1)
- Alpha and Omega (Revelation 1:8)
- Pioneer and perfecter of our faith (Hebrews 12:2)
- Bread of life (John 6:35)
- Chief Shepherd (1 Peter 5:4)
- The Christ (1 John 2:22)
- Faithful and true witness (Revelation 3:14)
- God (John 1:1; Hebrews 1:8; Romans 9:5)
- Great high priest (Hebrews 4:14)
- Horn of salvation (Luke 1:69)
- I am (John 8:58)
- King of kings, and Lord of Lords (Revelation 19:16)
- Lamb of God (John 1:29)
- Last Adam (1 Corinthians 15:45)
- Light of the world (John 8:12)
- Lion of the tribe of Judah (Revelation 5:5)
- Mediator (1 Timothy 2:5)
- Anointed One (or Messiah, Daniel 9:25–26)
- Mighty God (Isaiah 9:6)
- Redeemer (Isaiah 54:5)
- Resurrection and life (John 11:25)
- Savior (Ephesians 5:23; 2 Peter 2:20)
- Son of God (John 1:49)
- Wonderful Counselor (Isaiah 9:6)
- The Word (John 1:1)

WORLD SPINS BACKWARDS?

SCRIPTURES REFERENCED:

2 KINGS 20:1–11; ISAIAH 38; 2 KINGS 18:1–8; NUMBERS 21:1–9; PHILIPPIANS 3:21

In the climax of the 1978 film *Superman*, an anguished "Man of Steel" tries to bring his beloved (and recently deceased) Lois Lane back to life by reversing the earth's rotation.

Faster than a speeding bullet, Superman zips around and around the equator, creating a drag that first slows, then ultimately changes, the earth's spin. Time goes backwards, Lois's demise is undone, and once again, truth, justice, and the American way prevail.

SEEMS LIKE I'VE HEARD THAT BEFORE. . .

Nearly three millennia earlier, God wrote a similar story line—though without all the overblown Hollywood drama. This "movie" starred Hezekiah, playing the role of king of Judah, and Isaiah, cast as God's prophet. The tension? Hezekiah is seriously ill and about to die. Let's pick up on the scene:

The thirty-nine-year-old king, languishing in bed with a lethal boil, gets a visit from Isaiah. The prophet brings bad news: "This is what the LORD says: Put your house in order, because you are going to die; you will not recover."

The prophet Isaiah brings good news to the very ill king Hezekiah, in a sixteenth-century painting by the Dutch painter Jacob de Backer.

One of the best kings in Judah's history, Hezekiah "did what was right in the eyes of the LORD," smashing the altars people had built to false gods, and even destroying the bronze serpent God had told Moses to make to save the wandering, snake-bitten Israelites some six hundred years earlier. By Hezekiah's time, the people were worshipping the sculpture.

Isaiah's news hit Hezekiah hard, and he couldn't hold back his tears. Rolling over to face the wall, Hezekiah pleaded with God. "Remember, LORD," he prayed, "how I have walked before you faithfully and with wholehearted devotion and have done what is good in your eyes."

Of course, God doesn't forget things like that, and He was moved by Hezekiah's emotion. Before Isaiah had left the king's palace, God gave him a new message: "I have heard your prayer and seen your tears; I will heal you." Three days later, God said, Hezekiah would be healthy again and should plan to visit the temple of the Lord. And then God gave Hezekiah a surprising bit of information, essentially the date of his death: "I will add fifteen years to your life."

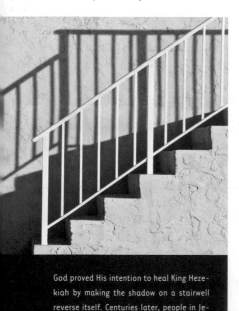

God proved His intention to heal King Hezekiah by making the shadow on a stairwell reverse itself. Centuries later, people in Jerusalem hoped the apostle Peter's shadow would touch the sick and heal them as he walked by (Acts 5:12–16).

GIVE ME A SIGN

Isaiah ordered the king's staff to whip up a cream of figs to apply to Hezekiah's boil, and the king immediately felt better. But Hezekiah wanted more proof that in three days' time he would indeed be able to worship at the temple. "Choose your own sign," God basically said, offering to make a shadow move either forward or backward ten steps on the palace stairway.

It's only a sign if it's something unusual, Hezekiah must have thought. So he answered Isaiah, "It is a simple matter for the shadow to go forward ten steps. . . . Rather, have it go back ten steps."

And that's exactly what happened.

Did the earth's spin actually reverse for a moment? Or was it just the shadow on the stairway breaking all the accepted rules of light and darkness? The Bible isn't clear on that question.

What is clear is that God can do whatever He pleases in the universe. The apostle Paul once wrote about God's power, the power of Jesus that "enables him to bring everything under his control."

Superman seems pretty wimpy in comparison.

HEZEKIAH: A RARE GODLY RULER

Hezekiah was that rare king of Judah who did right in God's eyes. He removed pagan worship from the kingdom and kept God's commandments. Under his command, the Levites cleansed the temple, and worship was restored. When the Assyrian king Sennacherib attacked Judah, Hezekiah gave him a large tribute.

Sennacherib sent officials to confer with Hezekiah's aides and try to convince his people to side with Sennacherib against their king and God. Sennacherib sent a message to Hezekiah belittling God and threatening Judah. Hezekiah brought the letter before God and asked Him to save Judah. Again, Isaiah prophesied the Assyrians' fall.

Sadly, Hezekiah followed the wicked King Ahaz, who led Judah into paganism, and preceded King Manasseh (his own son), who went so far as to erect pagan altars in the temple in Jerusalem. The Lord caused the Assyrian army to capture Manasseh and bring him to Babylon. Manasseh repented, and God brought him back to Jerusalem. He removed the idols from Jerusalem, repaired God's altar, and commanded his nation to follow God.

King Hezekiah, as envisioned by an unknown, seventeenth-century Swedish painter.

WHAT DO YOU CALL THEM?

SCRIPTURES REFERENCED:
ACTS 9:1–2; JOHN 14:6; ACTS 24:1–14; ACTS 11:26; REVELATION 3:7–13

Over the years, Christians have been called by many names—not all of them nice. Some, though, have been more descriptive than disparaging.

JUST DON'T CALL ME LATE FOR DINNER

Consider one of the first terms used to describe the early church: *the Way.* When you think about it, it makes sense—Jesus once described Himself as "the way and the truth and the life."

The first time we see that term, the persecutor Saul is planning a trip to Damascus, "so that if he found any there who belonged to the Way. . .he might take them as prisoners to Jerusalem." On his way to stop the Way, Saul was waylaid—by the Way and the Truth and the Life Himself. Jesus' intervention ended Saul's mission of death, starting a mission of life and peace. The persecutor-turned-pastor would later say boldly, during a trial before the Roman governor Felix, "I worship the God of our ancestors as a follower of the Way."

But Saul (better known by his later name, Paul) may have helped create the name by which believers are best known: *Christians.* The persecution Paul once encouraged had scattered Jewish believers beyond Jerusalem to

The Orontes River flows through modern Antakya, Turkey, the biblical city of Antioch where followers of Jesus first got the name "Christians."

MOST COMMON MEN'S NAMES IN THE BIBLE

Azariah (28 men)
Zechariah (27 men)
Shemaiah (25 men)
Maaseiah (21 men)
Meshullam (21 men)
Shimei (18 men)
Hananiah (14 men)
Hashabiah (14 men)
Joel (14 men)
Jonathan (14 men)
Shallum (14 men)
Jehiel (13 men)
Obadiah (13 men)
Benaiah (12 men)
Zichri (12 men)
Eliezer (11 men)
Johanan (11 men)
Joseph (11 men)
Bani (10 men)
Eliel (10 men)
Michael (10 men)
Nathan (10 men)
Nethaneel (10 men)

outlying areas such as Phoenicia, Cyprus, and Antioch. In the latter town, believers spread the good news to anyone who would listen—including non-Jews—and many turned to God through Jesus.

Back in Jerusalem, the news from Antioch was so encouraging that church leaders wanted to know more. They tabbed Barnabas for a fact-finding mission, and he found a thriving young church in need of some teaching. So Barnabas grabbed Saul, and for the next year, the two of them instructed the new believers in Antioch. Somewhere in that time, someone there came up with a new name for their little band: *Christians.*

Even today, that's the most common moniker for Jesus' followers—but a time will come when yet another name will apply.

KEEPING US IN SUSPENSE

In the book of Revelation, Jesus had words of praise, criticism, and challenge for seven churches of Asia Minor. To one of those churches, in Philadelphia, He said, "The one who is victorious I will make a pillar in the temple of my God. . . . I will write on them the name of my God. . .I will also write on them my new name."

What is that name, you ask? We don't know yet. You'll just have to stay tuned.

One of the best-known of the Bible's 28 Azariahs was the friend of Daniel ultimately known as Abednego. This Azariah had his name changed by the Babylonians, who had conquered Judah and carried many of its most promising citizens into exile.

NAMES/TITLES FOR BELIEVERS IN THE BIBLE

- Believers (1 Timothy 4:12)
- Blessed by my Father (Matthew 25:34)
- Brothers and sisters (Acts 12:17)
- Called to belong to Jesus Christ (Romans 1:6)
- Children of God (John 1:12; Philippians 2:15; 1 John 3:1–2) (John 11:52, 1 John 3:10)
- Children of light (Ephesians 5:8)
- Children of the living God (Romans 9:26)
- Children of the Most High (Luke 6:35)
- Children of the promise (Romans 9:8)
- Children of the resurrection (Luke 20:36)
- Chosen people (1 Peter 2:9)
- Christians (Acts 11:26, 26:28)
- Co-heirs with Christ (Romans 8:17)
- Dear brothers and sisters (1 Corinthians 15:58; James 2:5)
- Faithful brothers and sisters in Christ (Colossians 1:2)
- Fellow citizens with God's people (Ephesians 2:19)
- God's chosen people (Colossians 3:12)
- Heirs of God (Romans 8:17)
- Heirs of what was promised (Hebrews 6:17)
- Heirs together with Israel (Ephesians 3:6)
- Holy nation (1 Peter 2:9)
- Holy priesthood (1 Peter 2:5)
- Instruments for special purposes (2 Timothy 2:21)
- Light of the world (Matthew 5:14)
- Loved by God (Romans 1:7)
- Members of Christ (1 Corinthians 6:15)
- Obedient children (1 Peter 1:14)
- Objects of his mercy (Romans 9:23)
- People holy to the LORD (Deuteronomy 14:2)
- People of God (Hebrews 4:9; 1 Peter 2:10)
- People of the kingdom (Matthew 13:38)
- People of the light (Luke 16:8)
- Pillars in the temple of my God (Revelation 3:12)
- Priests to serve his God and Father (Revelation 1:6)
- Royal priesthood (1 Peter 2:9)
- Salt of the earth (Matthew 5:13)
- Slaves of Christ (1 Corinthians 7:22; Ephesians 6:6)
- Slaves to righteousness (Romans 6:18)
- The godly (2 Peter 2:9)
- The Lord's freed person (1 Corinthians 7:22)
- Those the LORD has rescued (Isaiah 51:11)
- Those who will inherit salvation (Hebrews 1:14)

Christians meet in "church buildings"—but every true believer in Jesus is part of *The Church*: "Christ is the head of the church, his body, of which he is the Savior" (Ephesians 5:23).

WHAT A WAY TO GO

SCRIPTURES REFERENCED:
GALATIANS 5:22–23; HEBREWS 9:27; JUDGES 4; JUDGES 9; 1 KINGS 21:23; 2 KINGS 9:7, 30–37; ACTS 12; 2 PETER 3:1–9

For a book that's ultimately about love, joy, peace, etc., the Bible records a lot of hideous, violent deaths. "People are destined to die once," the author of Hebrews wrote—but we can all hope we don't have to die like Sisera, Abimelek, Jezebel, or King Herod.

NAILED HIM!

Sisera was a military commander for the king of Hazor, leading a seemingly invincible army—including nine hundred iron chariots—against the Israelites. At that time, Israel was ruled by a "judge," or deliverer, and this one happened to be a woman named Deborah. It would be another woman, Jael, who would prove to be Sisera's downfall.

After God led a rout of Sisera's army—every one of his men was killed—the commander ran for his life, finding the tent of a man named Heber, whose family had been friendly with Hazor's king. Heber's wife, Jael, welcomed Sisera into the tent and encouraged him to rest from the day's exertions—putting a blanket over him and bringing him milk to drink. In those days before refrigerators, it was undoubtedly *warm* milk, and before long, big, tough Sisera was sleeping like a baby.

Sleeping babies are adorable—but there was nothing cute about Jael's next move. Sneaking up to the exhausted military man, she placed a tent peg against his temple and hammered it home to the ground below.

Sisera's gruesome death fulfilled a prophecy Deborah had uttered a short time before. Her military commander, Barak, had refused to engage Sisera's army unless Deborah went with him. She agreed but told Barak that he'd miss out on the glory of the coming victory: "Because of the course you are taking, the honor will not be yours, for the LORD will deliver Sisera

In fulfillment of Deborah's prophecy, a woman—Jael—claims victory over the military commander Sisera. The painting is by Italian artist Palma Giovane (1548–1628).

into the hands of a woman." That's exactly what happened—and Sisera wins our first "What a Way to Go" award.

I NEED SOME EXCEDRIN

Winner number two is another head-wound victim from the time of the judges: Abimelek. He was a son of Gideon, the man with the miracle fleece who led Israel against their enemies from Midian. Gideon was a man of great energy, leading a successful military campaign and still finding the time to father seventy (yes, *seventy*) sons.

Abimelek was one of those boys, born to a slave-woman concubine in a town named Shechem. Like boys today who dream of becoming president, Abimelek fancied himself king. Convincing his fellow Shechemites that he was their guy, Abimelek got himself crowned—shortly after killing all but one of his brothers.

That kind of crime can't go unpunished, and God made sure that Abimelek got what was coming to him. At the Lord's instigation, some residents of Shechem turned against Abimelek, starting a kind of civil war. In one of the ensuing battles, Abimelek chased the people of nearby Thebez into the city's tower, preparing to burn the structure—and everyone in it—to the ground. But as he carried fire to the doorway, a woman on the roof got Abimelek in her crosshairs, dropping an upper millstone onto his head.

That sounds like a miserable way to die, but the stone missile didn't actually kill Abimelek—it only cracked his skull. Though the wound was likely to have caused the king's death, he still had the mental capacity to worry about what people would think of him. "Draw your sword and kill me," he ordered his armor bearer, "so that they can't say, 'A woman killed him.'"

Silly pride? Perhaps. But whoever was responsible for Abimelek's demise, the end result was the same: He was dead. Ditto for Jezebel, after masterminding the murder of an innocent man for his vineyard (see "Government Runs Amok" on page 68).

SHE HAD IT COMING

The husband-bossing, idol-worshipping, farmer-killing queen of Israel was cruising for a bruising with the Lord, who didn't appreciate much of *anything* she did. God delivered his verdict on Jezebel through His prophet Elijah: "Concerning Jezebel the LORD says: 'Dogs will devour Jezebel by the wall of Jezreel.'" For becoming human Alpo, Jezebel wins the third "What a Way to Go" award.

At this point, Israel had a new king, Jehu, freshly anointed by a prophet who gave him God's instructions: "You are to destroy the house of Ahab your master, and I will avenge the blood of my servants the prophets and the blood of all the LORD's servants shed by Jezebel." Judgment fell on Jezebel (actually, Jezebel fell to judgment) exactly where God had said, at Jezreel.

Jehu came looking for Jezebel, who, in her characteristically haughty way, had done her hair and makeup to look good for the confrontation. From an upper window, Jezebel shouted an insult at Jehu, who then called out to the household servants, "Who is on my side? Who?" When a couple of eunuchs appeared at the window, Jehu commanded them to throw Jezebel down. And they did—fulfilling the idle daydreams of countless employees with cranky bosses.

Seriously wounded in the fall, Jezebel was finished off by horses that trampled her underfoot. And if that isn't grisly enough for you, get a load of this: in

A re-enactor in Nazareth, Israel, leads a donkey in pressing olives with a millstone. The "upper millstone" that cracked Abimelek's skull may not have been this large (that would have taken quite a lady to heft it), but any item dropped from a height can really smart.

Palace servants toss the boss—Jezebel—out the window, in another nineteenth-century woodcut by Gustave Doré.

fulfillment of God's prophecy, dogs ate everything but Jezebel's head, feet, and hands.

Okay, so it would be really rude to ask Jezebel, "What's eating you?" But anyone so inclined could ask the same question of Herod, king of Judea in the days of the early church.

EWWWW. . . .

Nastiness ran in the man's genes: His father, Herod Antipas, had killed John the Baptist and mocked Christ at His trial, and his grandfather, known as Herod the Great, had been anything but great when killing the baby boys of Bethlehem in his attempt to rub out young Jesus.

This particular Herod, known to history as Herod Agrippa I, continued the family history of murder by having the apostle James, the brother of the apostle John, killed with a sword. Then he arrested Peter, apparently planning the same fate for him. God didn't allow that, sending an angel to break Peter out of prison.

Herod was really pushing the limits of God's patience, and when he actually stepped over the line, the results were gruesome.

Some of Herod's subjects needed more food, so they begged an audience with the king. Herod agreed to meet with them and, dressed in his royal finery, provided the hungry audience with a kingly speech. Figuring flattery was the quickest way to the king's heart (and to filling their own stomachs), the listeners responded by yelling, "This is the voice of a god, not of a man."

Herod loved it—very briefly. "Immediately, because Herod did not give praise to

Herod Agrippa I appears on a bronze coin from the first century AD. The coin sold at auction for $5,300 in 2008.

God, an angel of the Lord struck him down, and he was eaten by worms and died."

Death by flesh-eating worms—and Herod Agrippa I wins our final "What a Way to Go" award.

EWWWW. . .GROSS! OTHER NASTY STUFF IN THE BIBLE (IN THE INIMITABLE LANGUAGE OF THE KING JAMES VERSION)

Boils (Job 2:7)
My breath is strange (Job 19:17)
Carcase of Jezebel (2 Kings 9:37)
Cut off his head (1 Samuel 17:51)
Dead men's bones (Matthew 23:27)
Dogs licked up his blood (1 Kings 22:38)
Eat their own dung (2 Kings 18:27)
Eaten of worms (Acts 12:23)
Emerods (1 Samuel 5:9)
Issue of blood (Luke 8:43)
Leprosy (Leviticus 13:25)
Lice upon man (Exodus 8:18)
Mildew (Haggai 2:17)
Put out his eyes (Judges 16:21)
Scab (Deuteronomy 28:27)
Swarms of flies (Exodus 8:29)
The land stank (Exodus 8:14)
Vomit (Proverbs 26:11)

In a seventeenth-century painting by Georges de la Tour, Job's wife urges her husband to "curse God and die" (Job 2:9) after Satan afflicts the good man with boils. Job's response? "You are talking like a foolish woman. Shall we accept good from God, and not trouble?" (Job 2:10).

BAD NEWS, GOOD NEWS

God's judgment can be severe, and there's more to come according to the apostle Peter: "The present heavens and earth are reserved for fire, being kept for the day of judgment and destruction of the ungodly." That's the bad news.

The good news is that God is in no hurry to wipe out people. Quite the opposite, actually. In Peter's words, God is "patient with you, not wanting anyone to perish, but everyone to come to repentance."

FISH COUGHS UP CASH

SCRIPTURES REFERENCED:
MATTHEW 17:24–27; MATTHEW 4:12–13; COLOSSIANS 1:16–17

What do you do when you owe money but have nothing on hand? You could ask for a payment extension or find a job to earn some cash. Some people choose to skip town. If you're Jesus, though, you perform a Bible marvel.

FEELS LIKE APRIL 15

It wasn't that Jesus had bought a flat-screen TV on credit and lacked the means to pay it off. His "debt" was a tax designed to support God's temple, and the collectors weren't about to let Jesus off the hook. A hook, though, would factor into the payment of the tax.

In Jesus' headquarters town of Capernaum, the tax collectors accosted Peter: "Doesn't your teacher pay the temple tax?" Peter assured them that Jesus did pay His taxes, then went to look for the man in question.

When Peter found Jesus, the Lord proved his supernatural knowledge by raising the issue even before Peter spoke. "What do you think, Simon?" Jesus asked. "From whom do the kings of the earth collect duty and taxes— from their own children or from others?"

Peter answered, "From others," and Jesus agreed that kings tended to exempt their own sons from taxation—hinting strongly that since He was God's Son, He shouldn't have to pay a tax to support His Father's temple.

"But so that we may not cause offense," Jesus added, giving Peter a unique quick-cash plan, "go to the lake and throw out your line. Take the first fish you catch; open its mouth and you will find a four-drachma coin. Take it and give it to them for my tax and yours."

Boats on the Sea of Galilee, near Jesus' adopted hometown of Capernaum. Jesus moved there from Nazareth, where Mary and Joseph had settled after their flight to Egypt to avoid King Herod's order to kill all young boys of Bethlehem (see Matthew 2).

THE LIFE AND MINISTRY OF THE APOSTLE PETER

- Named Simon son of Jonah; Jesus later called him Peter (Matthew 16:17; Luke 6:14)
- Peter and his brother Andrew came from Bethsaida, a fishing village on the Sea of Galilee, where they worked as fishermen (John 1:44; Matthew 4:18)
- Jesus called Peter and Andrew to follow Him, and He would make them "fish for people" (Matthew 4:18–19)
- Peter, though he was often impulsive and spoke inappropriately, was the leader among the twelve apostles
- At Jesus' invitation Peter attempted to walk on the water of the Sea of Galilee (Matthew 14:29–30)
- Peter, James, and John were Jesus' closest disciples and were with Him at the mountain during the Transfiguration and at Gethsemane on the night of His arrest (Mark 9:2)

- Peter confessed Jesus as the Christ at Caesarea Philippi (Mark 8:27–30)
- In the Garden of Gethsemane, Peter attempted to defend Jesus and cut off the ear of Malchus (John 18:10–11)
- Following Jesus' arrest, Peter denied his Lord three times in the courtyard of the high priest in Jerusalem (John 18:25–27)
- Following the giving of the Great Commission, Peter spoke out boldly in his Pentecost sermon (Acts 2:14–36)
- Peter healed the lame beggar at the temple gate and refused to stop preaching when the Jewish Council arrested him (Acts 3–5)
- Peter had a vision about the acceptance of Gentile believers in the church (Acts 10:1–43)

HOW ON EARTH. . .

The Bible never explains how the money got there. Did God cause the coin to materialize inside the mouth of the creature? Or had a fisherman

Creating a coin from nothing would be an impressive thing; creating a live fish even more so. But Jesus was the Word the whole world was made through (see John 1:1–3). That's a lot of coins, fish. . .and everything else.

Jonah turned biblical fishing on its head, when the underwater creature caught *him*. Jesus later used Jonah's three-day stay in the fish's stomach as a picture of the time He would be in the grave before the Resurrection (Mntthew 12:39 40).

FISH AND FISHING IN THE BIBLE

Genesis 1:26, 28—Among the creatures over which man would have dominion

Exodus 7:18–21—The fish in the Nile River died when the river's water turned to blood

Numbers 11:5—The people of Israel often ate fish while they were in Egypt

Jonah 1:17—God prepared a great fish to swallow Jonah, who would stay in the creature's belly for three days and three nights

Jonah 2:10—At God's command, the great fish He had prepared vomited Jonah onto dry land

Matthew 4:18–22—Jesus calls Simon Peter, Andrew, James, and John—all fishermen by trade—to follow Him and be His apostles

Luke 5:4–11—A miraculous catch of fish

Matthew 14:13–21—Jesus feeds 5,000 with five loaves of bread and two fish

Matthew 15:29–38—Jesus feeds 4,000 with seven loaves of bread and a few fish

Matthew 17:27—Jesus instructed Peter to cast out his line, and the first fish the apostle would bring in would have the money they needed for a temple tax

Luke 24:42–43—After Jesus' resurrection, the apostles gave him some broiled fish, which He ate in front of them

John 21:1–8—Another miraculous catch of fish

John 21:9–13—Jesus and the disciples dine on fish and bread on the seashore

accidentally dropped a coin, the movement of which through the water caught the eye of a hungry fish?

If the latter, the story is no less miraculous: Jesus still had to know about the coin (as well as its denomination), and Peter's line had to bring up the one fish in the Sea of Galilee that could solve Jesus' "problem."

Of course, Jesus never really had a problem—He knew exactly what was going to happen and how to fix it. And why not? According to the apostle Paul, "For in him all things were created: things in heaven and on earth, visible and invisible, whether thrones or powers or rulers or authorities; all things have been created through him and for him. He is before all things, and in him all things hold together."

HOW MANY ANIMALS ON THE ARK?

SCRIPTURES REFERENCED:
GENESIS 6:1–9:17; LEVITICUS 11

A quick quiz, dear reader: How many of each kind of animal did Noah have on the ark?

That's easy, you say—two. From your earliest days, you remember the Noah's ark wallpaper in your room at home. . .or the Noah's ark toys in the church nursery. . .or the Noah's ark picture books you read—each one showing a *pair* of animals. Two elephants. Two giraffes. Two zebras. Two duck-billed platypuses. Well, you get the idea.

Some speculate that Noah took young (read: smaller) animals on the ark to conserve space. Makes sense with elephants, which can reach 13 feet in height and weigh more than seven tons.

TWELVE SHORT?

Would you be surprised to learn that Noah actually had *fourteen* of many kinds of animals on the ark? God spoke to Noah twice before the rains came down, the first time mentioning those familiar pairs of animals: "You are to bring into the ark two of all living creatures, male and female, to keep them alive with you."

The next time God spoke, He elaborated on His plan for Noah: "Take with you *seven pairs* of every kind of clean animal, a male and its mate, and one pair of every kind of unclean animal. . .and also *seven pairs* of every kind of bird, male and female, to keep their various kinds alive throughout the earth" (emphasis added). Seven pairs of birds and "clean" animals (in

Snow-capped Mt. Ararat brushes the clouds above Turkey. Many believe Noah landed on this peak, though the Bible account says the ark came to rest on the "mountains of Ararat" (Genesis 8:4), indicating it could have been elsewhere in the entire mountain range.

SOME IMPORTANT BIBLICAL MOUNTAINS

- **Mt. Ararat**—The mountain or mountains where Noah's ark came to rest following the great flood (Genesis 8:4).

- **Mt. Carmel**—The scene where Elijah confronted Ahab, king of Israel, and the priests of Baal (1 Kings 18:19–42).

- **Mt. Gerizim**—A mountain in Samaria, near Shechem, where the Israelite leaders were to bless the people after they entered the Promised Land (Deuteronomy 11:29–30).

- **Mt. Gilboa**—Here, the Philistines fought and killed the Israelites in their last battle with King Saul. King Saul's sons died in battle. When the king realized he would lose the battle, he killed himself there (1 Samuel 31:1–4).

- **Mt. Moriah**—Moriah is the land where God sent Abraham to sacrifice his son Isaac, then provided a ram for the sacrifice instead (Genesis 22).

- **Mt. Nebo (Pisgah)**—On Pisgah, Moses climbed to a vantage point from which he could view the Promised Land just before he died (Deuteronomy 34:1–3).

- **Mt. Olivet (Mount of Olives)**—A mountain ridge east of Jerusalem. Luke describes it as "a Sabbath day's journey" outside the city. From here Jesus ascended into heaven (Acts 1:12).

- **Mt. Sinai**—One day, God spoke to Moses from a burning bush near this mountain and called him to go back to Egypt and lead the Israelites out of slavery. "Though the bush was on fire it did not burn up" (Exodus 3:1–9).

- **Mt. Tabor**—Through Deborah, God commanded Barak to draw up to Mount Tabor before engaging in battle with Sisera, commander of the Canaanites (Judges 4).

- **Mt. Zion**—Originally the name for a fortified mound on one of Jerusalem's southern hills, Zion, or Mount Zion, became the name for the temple mount, then the city of Jerusalem, and was even sometimes applied to the whole nation of Israel (Joel 2:32).

other words, those that could be eaten, according to God's laws) make for fourteen representatives of many species on the ark.

A week later, the perfect storm let loose, and Noah and his menagerie rode out 40 days of rain and another 110 days of flood. When the ark finally landed on the mountains of Ararat, each of those animals was free to wander away and repopulate the earth with its mate.

OH, SO THAT'S WHY...

Well, not quite *all* of them walked away: "Then Noah built an altar to the Lord and, taking some of all the clean animals and clean birds, he sacrificed burnt offerings on it."

We can all be thankful for those crispy critters. When God smelled the "pleasing aroma" of the burnt offering, He decided that He would never again curse the ground for man's sin or destroy all living creatures with a flood. He even created a visual aid to help everyone remember His promise: "Whenever I bring clouds over the earth and the rainbow appears in the clouds, I will remember my covenant between me and you and all living creatures of every kind. Never again will the waters become a flood to destroy all life."

A BIBLICAL FIRST

Genesis 8:20—"Then Noah built an altar to the Lord and, taking some of all the clean animals and clean birds, he sacrificed burnt offerings on it"—is the first reference to an altar in the entire Bible.

An altar is one of several places of worship (as well as the tabernacle, the temple, the synagogue, and the church) listed in the Bible. An altar is a structure where sacrifices to God were offered during Old Testament times. Abraham erected altars in several places he visited (see Genesis 12:7–8; 13:18; 22:9) and also constructed an altar upon which he intended to sacrifice his son Isaac. Jacob, Moses, Joshua, Samuel, David, and other men of God also built altars.

Under a rainbow—the sign of God's promise to never again destroy the earth by water—Noah and his family make a sacrifice. The nineteenth-century painting is by Joseph Anton Koch.

SIBLING RIVALRY TO THE EXTREME

SCRIPTURES REFERENCED:

NUMBERS 12:1–15; ACTS 7:23–34; GENESIS 37, 39–45; GENESIS 4; PSALM 133:1

F orget Jan and Marsha from *The Brady Bunch* or the Barone brothers from *Everybody Loves Raymond*. Sibling rivalry, TV-style, can't hold a candle to the real deal in the Bible.

SHOULDA KNOWN BETTER

Take, for instance, Moses' brother and sister. Aaron and Miriam, it seemed, couldn't imagine their brother being the leader of the Israelites. After all, he was the baby of the family, you know—only eighty-some years old.

Actually, an in-law situation set off this bout of sibling contention. Aaron and Miriam didn't care for Moses' wife, a woman of African ancestry. The bad-mouthing of the poor girl soon advanced to a questioning of Moses' spiritual calling. "Has the LORD spoken only through Moses?" they asked. "Hasn't he also spoken through us?"

God would speak for Himself—very clearly—when He immediately called the group to the principal's office: "Come out to the tent of meeting, all three of you," God commanded. At that point, the Lord revealed Himself in a pillar of cloud near the tabernacle entrance and gave Aaron and Miriam a good dressing-down.

Miriam in happier days, playing a timbrel to celebrate the Israelites' escape from Egypt (see Exodus 15). Later, she'll incur God's anger for questioning Moses' leadership.

"When there is a prophet among you, I, the LORD, reveal myself to them in visions, I speak to them in dreams," God growled. "But this is not true of my servant Moses. . . . With him I speak face to face, clearly and not in riddles; he sees the form of the LORD. Why then were you not afraid to speak against my servant Moses?"

Furious, God took His cloud and left—at which point Aaron noticed that Miriam had turned white. It wasn't fear, though she must have been terrified. It was leprosy, a dreaded disease of the skin. "Please, my lord," Aaron blurted to Moses, "I ask you not to hold against us the sin we have so foolishly committed."

Without hesitation, Moses prayed, "Please, God, heal her!" And just like that, he defused a potential time bomb of resentment and rivalry.

DADDY'S BOY

Another Old Testament character took the high road with his decidedly low-road siblings: Joseph forgave the ten older brothers who sold him into slavery. These guys, at least, could argue provocation. While Moses was described as meek, "more humble than anyone else on the face of the earth," seventeen-year-old Joseph seemed to revel in his position as favorite son.

That's not the figurative term for a presidential candidate, but the reality of coddling by the patriarch Jacob, who "loved Joseph more than any of his other sons, because he had been born to him in his old age." That favoritism shone like Las Vegas neon when Jacob made Joseph a special, richly ornamented "coat of many colors" (KJV).

Joseph had been known to tattle on his big brothers, and when he had a dream of himself ruling over his entire family—and told them all about it—it was the

Joseph got a "coat of many colours" (Genesis 37:3), according to the King James Version of the Bible, first published in 1611. Modern translations often don't mention colors, using words like "special," "beautiful," or "ornate" to describe the robe. Whatever the original language meant exactly, Joseph's robe was a source of irritation to his brothers.

proverbial straw that. . .well, you know.

The older brothers saw an opportunity for revenge one day as they grazed sheep near a town called Dothan. On a fact-finding mission from Dad, Joseph tracked down his older siblings, who fired up the rivalry by plotting to kill the teen. The oldest (and in this case, wisest) brother, Reuben, argued against fratricide, suggesting that the brothers simply toss Joseph down a dry well instead.

That's exactly where Joseph ended up, after being stripped of his flashy togs. Reuben's secret plan to pull Joseph back out of the well and take him home to Daddy was dashed when the other brothers saw a caravan of merchants on their way to Egypt. So, for about a half pound of silver, Joseph was sold into slavery. . .and launched on an amazing trajectory that landed him in the number two spot of the Egyptian government, sort of a junior pharaoh.

The modern landscape of ancient Dothan

AN IMPORTANT BIBLICAL SITE

Dothan is not just the place where Joseph's brothers pastured their sheep and sold him into slavery but also the home of the prophet Elisha. It was here that Elisha prayed that the soldiers of the huge, advancing Syrian army would be struck with blindness (2 Kings 6:8–18). Later, the Syrian soldiers were cured of their blindness in Samaria (2 King 6:20).

One of Egypt's best-known pharaohs—King Tutankhamen, who ruled in the 1300s BC, a few hundred years after Joseph served the unnamed pharaoh of the Bible account.

You can read the whole story in Genesis 39, 40, and 41, but for our purposes, know that more than twenty years later, a famine struck the region, causing Joseph's father and brothers to begin scouting for food supplies. Egypt had plenty of chow, thanks to Joseph's wise leadership, and the brothers ultimately made their way to his palace to beg for help.

Joseph immediately recognized his siblings, though they had no clue that the powerful man before them was their once annoying little brother. The almost-a-pharaoh toyed with his brothers for a while—accusing them of spying, demanding that they bring back a younger brother they'd mentioned, putting valuables into the bags of grain the men had bought, making it appear as if they were thieves.

When Joseph finally revealed his true identity, the brothers were terrified. It was bad enough dealing with a powerful world leader. . .but to know he was their own brother, one they'd thrown into a pit and sold into slavery? *Uh-oh. . .* As with Moses, however, Joseph chose to leave the rivalry behind and forgive.

CSI: EDEN

There would be no forgiveness in the rivalry between the brothers Cain and Abel—since it's tough to forgive when you're dead. Poor Abel, the world's first little brother, became the world's first murder victim.

When one-fourth of the earth's total population (Adam, Eve, Cain, and Abel) turned up dead, God Himself had to play the role of crime scene investigator. The older brother, in the first suspect interview, came across suspiciously, answering God's question, "Where is your brother Abel?" with an unconvincing, "I don't know. . . . Am I my brother's keeper?"

Abel lies slain, at the hand of his brother Cain, in a marble statue in the Hermitage museum in St. Petersburg, Russia.

Next, God turned to the evidence: a definite blood stain in the field where Abel had last been seen alive. "What have you done?" God pressed Cain again. "Listen! Your brother's blood cries out to me from the ground."

Cain's motive? Extreme jealousy. It seems that God preferred Abel's offerings of animal fat to Cain's gifts of fruit—and Cain was ticked. God's response, though, shows that Cain *knew* what offering he was supposed to bring: "Why are you angry? Why is your face downcast? If you do what is right, will you not be accepted?" God asked.

Well, of course, he would have been. But, as God warned Cain, "sin is crouching at your door"—and Cain chose to do his own thing. Sadly, that sin birthed humanity's first case of sibling rivalry, which exploded into humanity's first homicide.

No wonder David wrote in the Psalms, "How good and pleasant it is when God's people live together in unity!"

ABEL IN THE HEBREWS 11 "FAITH HALL OF FAME"

Abel was the first Old Testament figure mentioned in Hebrews 11 as a member of what has come to be known as the "Faith Hall of Fame" (see verse 4). This chapter lists several men and women who set examples of what a life of faith looks like. Here are the others:

- Enoch (verse 5)
- Noah (verse 7)
- Abraham (verse 8, 17)
- Isaac (verse 20)
- Jacob (verse 21)
- Joseph (verse 22)
- Moses (verse 24–27)
- Rahab (verse 31)
- Gideon (verse 32)
- Barak (verse 32)
- Sampson (verse 32)
- Jephthah (verse 32)
- David (verse 32)
- Samuel (verse 32)
- The prophets (verse 32)

SUCCESSFUL TELEPORTATION

SCRIPTURES REFERENCED:
JOHN 20:19–20; JOHN 14:12; ACTS 8:36–40; 2 CORINTHIANS 11:24–25; 2 CORINTHIANS
12:2–4; 1 THESSALONIANS 4:16–17; 1 CORINTHIANS 15:51–52

B eam me up, Scotty."

With that phrase, or some variation thereof, characters in the old *Star Trek* television series could be "teleported" to most any spot they chose. A little molecular disassembly here, some reassembly there—and the crew of the Starship *Enterprise* could travel where no man had gone before with a minimum of time and absolutely no vehicle. Though the actual *how* of teleportation was left to the viewers' imagination, the idea was enthralling.

It was also two thousand years behind the times.

BIBLICAL BEAMERS

As is always the case, God has the good ideas before anyone else—and the New Testament records several instances of *biblical* teleportation. Jesus Himself tried it out first.

Newly resurrected, the Lord went looking for His disciples—and found them barricaded in a room together, fearing the angry mob that had crucified Jesus just days earlier. Like the stone of His tomb, the locked doors posed no obstacle to Jesus, who simply materialized in the presence of His friends, greeting the group with a hearty "Peace be with you!"

Less than a week before, Jesus had told His disciple Philip that anyone who had faith in Christ would perform miracles like Jesus had done—and "even greater things than these." Another believer named Philip, one of the church's first deacons, would prove those words true.

Prompted by God's Spirit, the latter Philip approached a chariot on the road going southwest out of Jerusalem. The rider, a government official from Ethiopia, was reading the book of Isaiah—and Philip explained that the words pointed to Jesus Christ. Understanding, conversion, and even baptism followed in rapid succession.

As Philip brought the Ethiopian out of the water, another case of biblical teleportation transpired: The evangelist was zapped by God's Spirit, not simply through a locked door, but several miles away to the town of Azotus. Unfazed by the experience, Philip resumed his preaching.

Another hard-to-stop preacher was teleported even farther—all the way to heaven. That would be Paul, the "takes a licking and keeps on ticking" apostle who overcame beatings, stoning, and shipwreck to carry the Gospel to the unsaved. At one point in his ministry, Paul was "caught up to paradise," where he "heard inexpressible things, things that no one is permitted to tell." Afterward, Paul was beamed back to earth, where he was given a "thorn in my flesh" to keep him humble.

An artist's conception of the rapture—when "the Lord himself will come down from heaven, with a loud command, with the voice of the archangel and with the trumpet call of God, and the dead in Christ will rise first. After that, we who are still alive and are left will be caught up together with them in the clouds to meet the Lord in the air" (1 Thessalonians 4:16–17).

WANNA TRY?

If a teleportation to heaven sounds cool, consider this: You might enjoy a similar ride someday. That's the word from Paul himself.

Writing to believers in Thessalonica and Corinth, the apostle looked ahead to the day Jesus would return to earth, coming "down from heaven, with a loud command, with the voice of the archangel and with the trumpet call of God." Instantaneously—in a flash, Paul said—dead Christians would burst out of their graves to meet Jesus in the air, with living Christians following quickly behind. "And so," Paul added, "we will be with the Lord forever."

One day, Jesus will beam His followers up—never to beam them back!

"I AM" STATEMENTS OF JESUS CHRIST

"I am the way and the truth and the life," Jesus said (John 14:6). . .and the ticket out of this earth for those who believe in Him. Here are several other "I am" statements Jesus made:

- The Messiah (John 4:25–26)
- I am the bread of life (John 6:35)
- I am the living bread (John 6:51)
- I am from [God] (John 7:29)
- I am the light of the world (John 8:12; 9:5)
- I am one who testifies for myself (John 8:18)
- I am from above (John 8:23)
- I am not of this world (John 8:23)
- Before Abraham was born, I am (John 8:58)
- I am the gate for the sheep (John 10:7)
- I am the good shepherd (John 10:11, 14)
- I am God's Son (John 10:36)
- I am the resurrection and the life (John 11:25)
- I am come into the world as a light (John 12:46)
- I am in the Father, and the Father is in me (John 14:10, 11)
- I am in my Father, and you are in me, and I am in you (John 14:20)
- I am the true vine (John 15:1)
- I am the vine (John 15:5)
- I am not of the world (John 17:14)
- I am the Alpha and the Omega (Revelation 1:8)
- I am the Alpha and the Omega, the First and the Last (Revelation 22:13)
- I am the Living One; I was dead, and now look, I am alive for ever and ever! (Revelation 1:18)
- I am he which searches hearts and minds (Revelation 2:23)
- I am the Root and the Offspring of David, and the bright Morning Star (Revelation 22:16)

MEN ESCAPE DEATH— PERMANENTLY

SCRIPTURES REFERENCED:
HEBREWS 9:27; GENESIS 5:1–24; 1 KINGS 17:7–24; 1 KINGS 18:16–40; 1 KINGS 19:19–21; 2 KINGS 2:1–17

Though he didn't write for the Bible, old Benjamin Franklin had some pretty keen insights. He really hit the nail on the head with that quip about the only sure things in life being death and taxes.

Well, taxes at least—because two biblical men were able to escape the "sure thing" of dying.

EXCEPTIONAL MEN

The Bible clearly teaches that death is the common denominator for everyone: "People are destined to die once, and after that to face judgment," said the writer of the book of Hebrews. Man or woman, rich or poor, tall or short, good-looking or homely as a mud fence, every person can expect a rendezvous with death.

But there were two biblical exceptions to this rule—guys by the names of Enoch and Elijah. They never died.

That's not to say they're still walking among us as five-thousand-year-old men. It is to say that God took them to heaven by extraordinary means, skipping the normal physical decline and cessation of body function. No, these two shot up to heaven with spirit, soul, and *body* intact.

NINE MIRACLES ASSOCIATED WITH ELIJAH

- Causing the rain the cease for three and a half years (1 Kings 17:1)
- Being fed by ravens (1 Kings 17:4)
- Maintaining a barrel of flour and jar of oil (1 Kings 17:14)
- Resurrecting the widow's son (1 Kings 17:22)
- Calling of fire from heaven on the altar at Mt. Carmel (1 Kings 18:38)
- Causing it to rain (1 Kings 18:45)
- Parting of the Jordan (2 Kings 2:8)
- Being caught up to heaven in a whirlwind (2 Kings 2:11)
- Appearing on the Mount of Transfiguration with Jesus (Luke 9:28–36)

The second alphabetically was the first to go. Just six generations removed from Adam, Enoch was a spry sixty-five-year-old when he fathered Methuselah, who would ultimately become the world's longest-living man (see "Man Lives Nearly a Thousand Years" on page 268). For the next three hundred years, Enoch fathered other sons and daughters, but more important, he "walked faithfully with God." Then one day he was gone—not dead, but physically transferred into eternity: "He was no more, because God took him away."

CHARIOT OF FIRE

That's all pretty dramatic, but nothing in comparison with Elijah's non-death. The great Old Testament prophet was well-known for miracles like raising a dead boy to life and calling down fire from heaven to expose the worthlessness of the false god Baal. When Elijah's time arrived, it would be an awe-inspiring, breathtaking show.

His time apparently was no secret. Twice, other prophets approached Elijah's protégé, Elisha (those names have confused generations of Sunday school students), to ask, "Do you know that the LORD is going to take your master from you today?" Elisha said he knew but preferred not to talk about it.

People must have talked, though, when the actual departure occurred. Elijah and Elisha were walking together when a flaming chariot—pulled by flaming horses—suddenly appeared on the scene. Bearing down on the pair, the chariot snagged Elijah on the way past, so quickly that the prophet's overcoat was torn away from him and left behind. The flaming conveyance then swirled its way to heaven on the updraft of a tornado. Elijah was gone, in style.

When people survive a serious accident, we often say they "escaped death." And perhaps they did, though only temporarily. But only Enoch and Elijah can say they escaped death forever.

"As [Elijah and Elisha] were walking along and talking together, suddenly a chariot of fire and horses of fire appeared and separated the two of them, and Elijah went up to heaven in a whirlwind" (2 Kings 2:11).

The great hope of heaven—of someday walking on streets of gold (Revelation 21:21)—relieves fear for those who follow Jesus.

COMFORTING MESSAGES FROM THE BIBLE ABOUT DEATH

- John 14:1–4: God has prepared a place for us in heaven, where we will spend eternity with Jesus Christ.
- Romans 8:16–17: Though we may suffer with him, one day we will be glorified by him.
- 2 Corinthians 5:6–8: To be away from the physical body means being in our eternal homes with God.
- 1 Thessalonians 4:16–18: Christ will return one day, and those who have died in Him will rise to meet Him first, followed by those who remain in their physical bodies.
- 1 Thessalonians 5:9–11: We should encourage one another in the fact that we won't face punishment when we die but God's eternal salvation.
- John 11:23–26: Those who believe in Jesus Christ, though they may die physically will never really die but live on eternally.
- 1 Corinthians 15:54–57: God has given us eternal victory over death through Jesus Christ.
- Philippians 3:20–21: Death means the transformation of our bodies into new, glorified bodies.
- 1 Corinthians 15:20–23: Christ has been raised from the dead, all who believe in Him will be made alive again—this time for eternity.
- Philippians 1:23–24: While we are alive, we can do more to further the kingdom of God, but when we die, we will be forever with Christ.
- 1 Peter 1:3–5: When we die, we receive a heavenly inheritance—and imperishable, undefiled, unfading, perfect inheritance that is being kept in heaven for us.
- John 10:27–29: In this life, we have the privilege of following Jesus; in the next life, we will never perish and nothing or no one can take us from Him.
- Romans 8:38–39: Death can never separate us from the love of God in Christ Jesus.
- Romans 14:8: In life or in death, we belong to the Lord.

GOD *HATES* PEOPLE?

SCRIPTURES REFERENCED:
ROMANS 5:8; 1 JOHN 4:8; GENESIS 6:5–6; JOHN 10:30; LUKE 23:34; PROVERBS 6:16–19

H ate the sin, love the sinner" is a little saying someone developed to describe God's approach to a messed-up humanity. While the Bible is clear that God hates sin of all sorts, it is also very clear that He loved people—all people— enough to send His only Son to die on the cross for them. The apostle John says love isn't just what God *does*, it's what He *is*. So it might come as a surprise to find that the Bible says God *hates* some people.

THAT'S SCARY. . .

It's not the people of Noah's time, who filled the earth with wickedness— God "regretted that he had made human beings on the earth, and his heart was deeply troubled." It's not the murderous, pagan nations that harassed His chosen people of Israel—though those nations were sometimes punished, pretty harshly, for their badness. It isn't even the Jerusalem mob, stirred up by jealous religious leaders, who put Jesus on a cross to die. As God's Son, who claimed "I and the Father are one," Jesus' response was "Father, forgive them." You'd have to count some of these people as the rottennest apples in human history, but the Bible never says God hated them. Who could be worse?

The answer to that question is found in Proverbs, in a list of "things the LORD hates. . .that are detestable to him." The first five are actually body parts, used to describe sinful tendencies: haughty eyes, a lying tongue, hands that shed innocent blood, a heart that devises wicked schemes, and feet that are quick to rush into evil. But the last two entries on the list are whole people: "a false witness who pours out lies and a person who stirs up conflict in the community."

"Hate the sin, *hate* the sinner" might be a more appropriate saying for people who lie and make trouble. Considering that a God of love can be brought to hatred by those two sins, it seems wise to avoid them.

"But God demonstrates his own love for us in this: While we were still sinners, Christ died for us" (Romans 5:8).

JESUS' SEVEN STATEMENTS FROM THE CROSS

- Pleading on behalf of His tormenters: "Father, forgive them, for they do not know what they are doing" (Luke 23:34).
- Praying to God the Father: "*Eli, Eli, lema sabachthani?*" (which means "My God, my God, why have you forsaken me?") (Matthew 27:46).
- Speaking to the penitent thief on the cross: "Truly I tell you, today you will be with me in paradise" (Luke 23:43).
- Speaking to His mother, Mary: "Woman, here is your son!" Speaking to the disciple He loved: "Here is your mother!" (John 19:26–27).
- "I am thirsty" (John 19:28).
- "Father, into your hands I commit my spirit" (Luke 23:46).
- "It is finished" (John 19:30).

FORTY DAYS WITHOUT FOOD?

SCRIPTURES REFERENCED:
ACTS 9:1–19; DANIEL 10:1–3; EXODUS 34:28; 1 KINGS 18:16–19:9; LUKE 3:22; LUKE
4:1–2; DEUTERONOMY 8:3; MATTHEW 4:1–11; MATTHEW 6:17–18

For those of us whose cupboards abound with Fritos, Oreos, and microwave popcorn; whose cars can't pass a McDonald's without zipping through the drive-through; whose clothing sizes tend to increase with each passing year, the idea of *fasting*— going without food for a period of time— is almost inconceivable.

AYE, AYE, SKIPPER

Skipping lunch would be a burden for many in our calorie-saturated society; bypassing food for an entire day could cause us to shrivel up and blow away in the wind. Well, not really—though we might want to think that.

The Bible, however, is full of fasts, and not just of the single-meal or single-day variety. The Christian persecutor turned Christian believer Saul skipped his food and water for three days after meeting Jesus on the road to Damascus. It was a three-*week* fast for the Old Testament prophet Daniel, troubled by a vision of the future. (The man who'd survived a night in a lions' den because of a miraculous fast by the big cats may have had *some* food during his twenty-one days of mourning. Daniel reported that he "ate no choice food; no meat or wine touched my lips.")

Could anyone fast longer than twenty-one days? You bet—and not just any*one*, but three.

These days we are most likely to refuse food if we are dieting. But for some, going without food is a way of focusing on our dependence on God.

OUR FIRST CONTESTANTS. . .

First in the hunger derby is Moses, high on Mount Sinai with God Himself. Making a return appearance on the big hill to pick up a duplicate set of the Ten Commandments (he'd shattered the first stone tablets in fury over the Israelites' sin with a golden calf), Moses spent forty days with the Lord "without eating bread or drinking water." That sounds miraculous—and it was. So was the prophet Elijah's forty-day experience in the time of the evil queen Jezebel.

Satan's third and final temptation of Jesus: After urging the Lord to break His fast by turning stones into bread, Satan next encouraged Jesus to jump off a high place of the temple, letting angels break His fall. Then the devil took Jesus to a high mountain, showing Jesus the beautiful view and pitching his ultimate diabolical dream: ""All this I will give you," he said, "if you will bow down and worship me" (Matthew 4:9). No dice.

After God skunked Baal at Mount Carmel (final score: Elijah 450, false prophets 0—see "Water Catches Fire!" on page 198), Jezebel threatened Elijah's life. Why that bothered him after what he'd just seen is a mystery—but Elijah turned yellow and ran. About a hundred miles later, when he finally stopped in Beersheba, Elijah asked God to kill him.

That was a prayer God chose to answer in the negative. Instead, He sent an angel with a fresh cake of bread ("angel food cake"?) and a jar of water. Like a modern teenager, Elijah got up to eat and drink. . .and then lay down again.

Persistence characterized the angel, though, who poked Elijah and urged him to eat some more. The great prophet did, and "strengthened by that food, he traveled forty days and forty nights until he reached Horeb, the mountain of God." Apparently traveling to the same mountain where Moses had met with God, Elijah faced a hike of about four hundred miles—and may have gone the entire distance on the strength of that one angelic meal.

Three-cornered hamantaschen (Jewish pastries) are eaten during Purim to celebrate Esther's victory over the evil Haman. Esther herself wasn't eating—she fasted before approaching her husband, King Ahasuerus, to alert him to Haman's plot.

BIBLICAL EXAMPLES OF PRAYER WITH FASTING— ABSTAINING FROM FOOD

- Jesus (Matthew 4:2)
- Moses (Exodus 34:28; Deuteronomy 9:9, 18)
- Elijah (1 Kings 19:8)
- The nation of Israel (Judges 20:26; Ezra 8:21; Esther 4:3)
- The Ninevites (Jonah 3:5–8)
- David (2 Samuel 12:16; Psalm 109:24)

- Nehemiah (Nehemiah 1:4)
- Esther (Esther 4:16)
- Daniel (Daniel 9:3)
- Disciples of John the Baptist (Matthew 9:14)
- Anna (Luke 2:37)
- The early Christians (Acts 13:2)

THE ULTIMATE EXAMPLE

Then there was Jesus, whose forty-day fast showed Satan who was boss.

Fresh off the spiritual high of His baptism, featuring a voice from heaven that proclaimed, "You are my Son, whom I love; with you I am well pleased," Jesus faced a major test: he was led by God's Spirit into the desert to be tempted by the devil.

It's bad enough to be singled out for temptation by Satan himself; compounding the trial was the fact that, for forty days, Jesus ate absolutely nothing. In a classic case of biblical understatement, Luke's Gospel notes, "At the end of [the forty days] he was hungry."

You bet He was—but Jesus was still in complete control of Himself, even when Satan struck at that gnawing feeling in the pit of Jesus' stomach. "If you are the Son of God," the devil sneered, "tell this stone to become bread." In other words, "Hey, Jesus, if you're so powerful, take my advice: turn a rock into food and forget this fasting stuff."

Of course, Jesus would *never* take a lead from Satan, no matter how tempting the idea might be. In this case, the Lord shot down the temptation with the big gun of scripture, reminding Satan of Moses' words to the people of Israel: "man shall not live by bread alone, but by every word of God" (KJV).

The devil lobbed two other temptations at Jesus, who swatted them away with additional scripture. Defeated, Satan slinked away, and angels came to "attend" to Jesus, the word hinting that they might have brought Him food. One would hope so—after forty days, He was due.

COME ON. . .REALLY?

But, you might ask, wouldn't it *kill* a person to go forty days—that's almost six weeks!—without food? A fast of that length would certainly be difficult, but it wouldn't necessarily be deadly: in 1981 an imprisoned Irish Republican named Bobby Sands staged a hunger strike that lasted sixty-six days until his death by starvation.

For Bobby Sands, fasting was a political statement; for Moses, Elijah, and Jesus, it was a spiritual service—and, we might add, a spiritual service that

God still blesses today. "When you fast," Jesus once said, "put oil on your head and wash your face, so that it will not be obvious to others that you are fasting, but only to your Father, who is unseen; and your Father, who sees what is done in secret, will reward you."

GOOD THINGS TO BRING WITH YOU WHEN YOU PRAY

- Repentance: "When your people Israel have been defeated by an enemy because they have sinned against you, and when they turn back to you and give praise to your name, praying and making supplication to you in this temple" (1 Kings 8:33; also see Jeremiah 36:7).
- Confession: "When I heard these things, I sat down and wept. For some days I mourned and fasted and prayed before the God of heaven" (Nehemiah 1:4; also see Nehemiah 1:7).
- Humility: "Then Abraham spoke up again: 'Now that I have been so bold as to speak to the Lord, though I am nothing but dust and ashes'" (Genesis 18:27).
- Weeping: "They will come with weeping; they will pray as I bring them back. I will lead them beside streams of water on a level path where they will not stumble, because I am Israel's father, and Ephraim is my firstborn son" (Jeremiah 31:9).
- Fasting: "When I heard these things, I sat down and wept. For some days I mourned and fasted and prayed before the God of heaven" (Nehemiah 1:4; also see Daniel 9:3; Acts 13:3).
- Watchfulness: "The end of all things is near. Therefore be alert and of sober mind so that you may pray" (1 Peter 4:7; also see Luke 21:36).
- Praise: "I cried out to him with my mouth; his praise was on my tongue" (Psalm 66:17).
- Thanksgiving: "Do not be anxious about anything, but in every situation, by prayer and petition, with thanksgiving, present your requests to God" (Philippians 4:6; also see Colossians 4:2).
- Persistence: "I tell you, even though he will not get up and give you the bread because of friendship, yet because of your shameless audacity he will surely get up and give you as much as you need" (Luke 11:8).

THE LOST LETTER OF PAUL

SCRIPTURES REFERENCED:

COLOSSIANS 4:16; 2 TIMOTHY 3:16; ISAIAH 40:8

Is the Bible a book? Of course, you say. It contains printed sheets of paper bound together under one cover.

Technically, though, the Bible is a *collection* of "books"—sixty-six separate writings that we know as Genesis, Exodus, Leviticus, etc., all the way through 3 John, Jude, and Revelation.

DROP ME A LINE

Many of the books of the Bible, especially those in the middle of the New Testament, are really letters. In the old-time language of the King James Version, they're known as *epistles*. (No, "epistles" aren't the wives of apostles.)

The apostle Paul wrote several epistles, both to individuals (1 and 2 Timothy, Titus, Philemon) and to churches (Romans, 1 and 2 Corinthians, Galatians, Ephesians, Philippians, Colossians, 1 and 2 Thessalonians, and Laodiceans).

What? You don't remember that last letter? Paul apparently composed one, according to his letter to the church at Colosse: "After this letter has been read to you, see that it is also read in the church of the Laodiceans and that you in turn read the letter from Laodicea."

The letter carriers who delivered Paul's epistles—walking, riding, and sailing between Israel, Turkey, and Italy—were likely men of faith and glad to be of service. No stamps required!

THE ONE THAT GOT AWAY

So why don't we have a biblical book of Laodiceans? Only God can say.

If, as Paul once wrote to Timothy, "All scripture is given by inspiration of God" (KJV), and if, as the prophet Isaiah once wrote, "The grass withers and the flowers fall, but the word of our God endures forever," then we have to assume that the letter to Laodicea wasn't on the same spiritual level as Paul's epistles to Rome, Corinth, Galatia, Ephesus, and so on.

But wouldn't it be interesting to know what it said?

IMPORTANT DATES (AND FACTS) IN COMPILING THE BOOKS OF THE BIBLE

- c. 1400 BC—The Ten Commandments delivered to Moses
- c. 500–400 BC—Completion of Hebrew manuscripts that would become the thirty-nine Old Testament books
- Third and Second centuries BC—Completion of the Septuagint, a translation of all thirty-nine books of the Old Testament canon and the 14 books of the Apocrypha into Greek
- 1st Century AD—Completion of all original manuscripts that make up the twenty-seven New Testament books
- c. 315—Athanasius, Bishop of Alexandria, identifies the 27 books of the New Testament
- c. 362—Council of Laodicea adopts canon of Old and New Testaments and the Apocrypha
- 393—Council of Hippo—Affirms canon of New Testament

A statue of Athanasius, the early church father who first identified the 27 books of the New Testament, outside a Danish church.

MEGADISASTERS

SCRIPTURES REFERENCED:
GENESIS 18–19; 2 PETER 2:6–8; 2 SAMUEL 24; NUMBERS 1:1–3; NUMBERS 26:1–2;
2 SAMUEL 8:11–16; PSALM 20:7; 2 KINGS 18–19; REVELATION 6, 9; 1 THESSALONIANS
4:13–18; 5:9

Hollywood regularly churns out disaster flicks to feed a public hunger for frightening "what ifs": What if space aliens obliterated the White House? What if a massive earthquake hurled California into the ocean? What if a nuclear bomb found its way into the wrong hands? What if the Chicago Cubs actually won the World Series?

Screenwriters may get inspiration from the newspaper headlines, or perhaps from deep in their own fevered imaginations. It's doubtful that many would turn to the pages of scripture, yet the Bible contains stories of calamities so massive they could truly be categorized as *mega*disasters.

SO LONG AND GOOD-BYE

Long before Minneapolis and St. Paul, Sodom and Gomorrah were the original Twin Cities. But you won't find Sodom and Gomorrah on any present-day maps—they hold the unenviable distinction of being wiped off the face of the earth by a very angry deity.

What so upset God? Maybe the fact that He couldn't find even *ten* good people in the whole city of Sodom—and Abraham had bargained God down to that point from an original target of fifty. The men of Sodom were so corrupt they even tried to molest the two angels God sent to warn the one righteous man of the city—Lot—to escape.

This rock formation overlooking the Dead Sea is called "Lot's Wife," a reference to the woman who looked back on God's destruction of her hometown of Sodom, and became a pillar of salt. Jesus used the unfortunate woman as an example to all believers to be ready for His second coming: "Remember Lot's wife!" (Luke 17:32).

THE LIFE OF ABRAHAM

- From Ur of the Chaldees to Haran—The death of his father, Terah (Genesis 11:31–32)
- From Haran to Shechem—Builds altar (Genesis 12:1–7)
- From Shechem to Bethel—Abraham and Lot offer sacrifices to God (Genesis 12:8)
- From Bethel to Egypt—Abraham denies Sarah is his wife (Genesis 12:10–16)
- From Egypt to Bethel—Abraham offers prayers (Genesis 13:1–4)
- From Bethel to Hebron—Builds altar and offers sacrifice (Genesis 13:18)
- From Hebron to Hobah—Abraham rescues Lot (Genesis 14:1–16)
- From Hobah to Hebron—Ishmael born; three angels give promise of a son; Sodom destroyed (Genesis 14:16–19:25)
- From Hebron to Gerar—Isaac born and presented to Abraham (Genesis 20:1–21:16)
- From Gerar to Beersheba—Abraham makes covenant with Abimelek (Genesis 21:31–34)
- From Beersheba to Mt. Moriah—Abraham willing to sacrifice Isaac but is stopped from doing so at the last moment (Genesis 22:1–18)
- From Mt. Moriah to Beersheba (Genesis 22:19)
- From Beersheba to Hebron—The death of his wife, Sarah (Genesis 23:1–2, 19–20)
- From Hebron to Beersheba—The death of Abraham at 175 years of age (Genesis 25:7–8)
- Isaac and Ishmael carry Abraham's body to Hebron (Genesis 25:9)

The structure in Hebron, built over the Cave of the Patriarchs—believed to be the tomb of Abraham.

Lot, his wife, and their two daughters made a reluctant retreat from Sodom, physically pulled along by the two angels. Shortly after sunrise on D-Day (*D* standing for *doom*), with Lot and his crew safely out of the way, God "rained down burning sulfur on Sodom and Gomorrah," destroying every person in the cities as well as all the plant life in the region.

The Bible never says how many people died in the catastrophe, but the number may have been in the thousands. Whatever the figure, you can add one more casualty: Lot's wife, who disregarded the angels' warning against looking back. When she cast a retro glance at her blazing hometown, she became "a pillar of salt."

ROUGH PUNISHMENT

We know exactly how many died in a megadisaster of King David's time: seventy thousand Israelites, from the northern part of the country to the southern regions, fell in a plague. Once again, an angry God was behind the calamity.

This time, the Israelites themselves weren't to blame—the king was. David had given in to temptation, and not his lust for Bathsheba. He decided to take a census.

What's wrong with that, you ask? To answer that question, we'll need to do some reading between the lines.

Years before, early in the Israelites' march out of Egyptian slavery, God had told Moses to count the people. At the end of their forty-year meander to the Promised Land, God told Moses to count them again. (Those tallies are described in the Bible's book of "Numbers"—get it?)

By David's time, and by God's grace, Israel was no longer a wandering clot of humanity, but a world power. The king's decision to count his people—especially the men of fighting age—struck David's military commander, Joab, as a tad foolish. "Why does my lord the king want to do such a thing?" the general asked.

Joab had seen plenty of military successes in his time, having conquered Edomites, Moabites, Ammonites, Amalekites, and Philistines (*-ines* not *-ites*), just to name a few. But Joab's hesitation to count the soldiers suggests that he may have seen God—rather than his own generalship—as the secret to Israel's victories. David, who at some time in his life wrote in the Psalms, "Some trust in chariots and some in horses, but we trust in the name of the LORD our God," may have been shifting his focus to human capabilities. That spiritual lapse would have deadly consequences.

As kings tend to do, David overruled Joab, and the various army officers began numbering their men. The count took almost ten months to complete, but David's realization of his sin seemed to occur immediately as Joab announced the total. "I have sinned greatly in what I have done," the king prayed. "Now, LORD, I beg you, take away the guilt of your servant. I have done a very foolish thing."

Foolish, indeed—because God demanded a heavy punishment. And David himself would choose the punishment.

Like a contestant on an ancient version of the game show *Let's Make a Deal*, David got three options—but they were all bad. "Shall there come on you three years of famine in your land?" the prophet Gad asked the king. "Or three months of fleeing from your enemies while they pursue you? Or three days of plague in your land?"

David mulled the options briefly, then decided on Door #3. "Let us fall into the hands of the LORD, for his mercy is great," David reasoned, "but do not let me fall into human hands."

God sent an angel of death to plague Israel, and seventy thousand people died before the Lord called a halt to the slaughter. David, whose sin started the catastrophe, watched in horror, saying, "I have sinned. . . . What have they done? Let your hand fall on me and my family."

IT GETS WORSE

God often handled His chosen people, the Israelites, harshly. That's because from top to bottom, from powerful king to lowest peasant, the Israelites often blew it with disobedience, disrespect, and distinctly dumb decisions. But God believes in equal-opportunity justice. Just ask the Assyrian army.

No, wait, you can't—the entire army is dead, all 185,000 soldiers in one fell swoop of God's wrath.

Around seven hundred years before Jesus, a man named Hezekiah ruled the southern Jewish nation of Judah. Though God's chosen people had had a lot of stinkeroo kings, Hezekiah was a good one: "He did what was right in the eyes of the LORD. . .trusted in the LORD. . .held fast to the LORD." All in all, "there was no one like him among all the kings of Judah, either before him or after him."

But being good won't protect a person from troubles. Hezekiah's trouble arrived in the form of an Assyrian emissary who stomped into Jerusalem with a snide speech threatening doom on the nation. The Assyrian even rudely predicted that Hezekiah's soldiers would have to eat and drink their own human waste to survive the deprivations ahead.

As a godly king should, Hezekiah took his problem to the Lord. Through the prophet Isaiah (the same guy who wrote that looong book in the Old Testament), God told Hezekiah, essentially, "Don't sweat it": "Do not be afraid of what you have heard—those words with which the underlings of the king of Assyria have blasphemed me."

The Assyrian king, Sennacherib, had crossed a line. "Who is it you have ridiculed and blasphemed?" God thundered through Isaiah. "Against whom have you raised your voice and lifted your eyes in pride? Against the Holy One of Israel!" Promising Hezekiah that the Assyrian king would never enter Jerusalem, God said he would send Sennacherib packing.

First, though, there was the issue of 185,000 enemy soldiers outside the city. *No problemo*, as God sent His angel to kill every one of them that very night. Sennacherib himself *wasn't* killed, but he awoke to a very nasty surprise—then beat a hasty retreat to his home in Nineveh. Sometime later the king of Assyria became God's 185,001st victim, when Sennacherib's own sons assassinated him.

This ancient painting depicts the healing of Hezekiah: The king was dying, he prayed earnestly to the Lord, and Isaiah informed him that God had granted him fifteen more years to live (2 Kings 20:1–11). Unfortunately, Isaiah also prophesied coming trouble with Assyria.

AND WORSE YET

If you think 185,000 deaths in one night is a major disaster, get a load of the frightful prophecies in the book of Revelation. A day is coming, John wrote, when God will break the seven seals on a scroll in heaven—and, wow, what a scary peck of problems they unveil!

Each of the first four seals reveals a colored horse and rider ("the four horsemen of the Apocalypse," if you've heard that phrase), who bring war, famine, and ultimately the death of *one-quarter* of the earth's people. Using today's global population as a guide, this seal judgment will kill some one and a half *billion* people.

And they won't die easily, either. A pale horse carrying a rider named Death will kill "by sword, famine and plague, and by the wild beasts of the earth." Soon afterward a worldwide cataclysm—including a massive earthquake, a meteorite bombardment, and the complete overturning of sky and land—will cause the surviving humans to cry out for death.

A third of them will get their wish when the sixth of God's "trumpet judgments" takes place. After hail, fire, and blood fall from heaven to earth (trumpet #1), a giant meteorite poisons the seas (trumpet #2), a comet poisons the rivers (trumpet #3), the sun, moon, and stars darken (trumpet #4), and locusts from hell invade the earth (trumpet #5), the next trumpet will summon a quartet of angels who will kill one-third of humanity—potentially another billion and a half people. That's a total death toll of *three billion*—the number three followed by *nine* zeros—clearly a disaster of the first order.

STUNNING, AIN'T IT?

Such inconceivable numbers overwhelm some people, who prefer simply not to think about them. Others get nervous, fearing they'll be caught up in "the end of the world"—and that they won't enjoy the experience.

But for Christians, it may be a moot point. The apostle Paul, in a letter to the believers in Thessalonica, wrote that "God did not appoint us to suffer wrath." In the context of his comments on the rapture, when "the dead in Christ will rise first" and "after that, we who are still alive and are left will be caught up together with them in the clouds to meet the Lord in the air," Paul seemed to be saying that Christians will be "outta here."

At that point, megadisasters are history. Everything is future, when "we will be with the Lord forever."

Thunderclouds threaten a Montana farm, in a scene reminiscent of the seventh plague on Egypt.

ONE DISASTER AFTER ANOTHER

When you think of the word *disaster* as it relates to the Bible, it's hard not to think of what happened to the Egyptians due to Pharaoh's stubbornness and refusal to grant the Israelites their freedom. Here are the ten disasters—also known as plagues—in the order they took place:

1. The Nile River water is turned to blood (Exodus 7:14–24)
2. Swarms of frogs (Exodus 8:1–15)
3. Gnats cover humans and animals (Exodus 8:16–19)
4. Swarms of flies fill the houses (Exodus 8:20–24)
5. Disease kills Egyptian livestock (Exodus 9:1–7)
6. Humans and animals are covered with sores (Exodus 9:8–12)
7. Hail, thunder, and rain knock down crops (Exodus 9:13–35)
8. Locusts eat the plants the hail and rain haven't knocked down (Exodus 10:1–20)
9. Darkness covers the land (Exodus 10:21–29)
10. Death of all firstborn Egyptian baby boys and animals (Exodus 12:1–30)

PROPHET BREAKS THE LAW—OF PHYSICS

SCRIPTURES REFERENCED:
2 KINGS 6:1–7; 2 KINGS 2:11–14; 2 KINGS 4:8–37; 2 KINGS 6:8–23

Sometime around seventh grade, most of us take a general science class. There we're exposed to some basic concepts of physics—things like magnetism, buoyancy, and all those formulas that make us say, "Huh?"

We can be fairly certain that the Bible's Elisha never took that class. More concerned with God than gravity, preaching than particles, and miracles than matter, the great prophet spent his time and energy on *spiritual* things. But in one brief episode, without batting an eye, he turned two physical laws on their heads.

PROBLEM, SOLUTION

It happened near the Jordan River, where Elisha was cutting down trees with a group of prophets he oversaw. The junior sages had plans to build themselves a new place to live, one large enough to accommodate their meetings with Elisha.

As one man swung back, the ax head flew off, arcing into the waters of the Jordan River. "Oh no, my lord," he cried out in dismay, "it was borrowed!"

No problem—there's a miracle man on the scene.

For a guy who'd seen his mentor Elijah taken to heaven in a whirlwind, who'd parted the Jordan River by striking it with Elijah's left-behind cloak,

No, they're not looking for a missing ax head—they're getting baptized in the Jordan River like Jesus did. The Jordan is a popular tourist site for visitors to the Holy Land.

and who'd raised a dead boy from Shunem back to life, recovering a submerged ax head was no big deal.

Elisha cut a stick and tossed it into the water. The piece of wood suddenly became magnetic, pulling the ax head upward. And the iron suddenly gained buoyancy, floating within reach of the prophet who'd lost it. "Lift it out" was Elisha's only comment.

Then he moved on to a bigger miracle—blinding an enemy army that had come to capture him.

This twelfth-century enamel plaque shows Naaman bathing in the Jordan. The hand sending down rays of power from the top right corner leaves us in no doubt as to the source of his healing.

OLD TESTAMENT MIRACLES AT THE JORDAN RIVER

- Israelites, under command of Joshua, cross on dry ground (Joshua 3:15–17)
- Elijah and Elisha cross the Jordan on dry ground (2 Kings 2:8)
- Elisha crosses by himself (2 Kings 2:14)
- God heals Naaman of leprosy by having him bathe in its waters (2 Kings 5:14)
- Elisha makes an ax head of one of the "children of the prophets" float (2 Kings 6:6)

A STRANGE, DISTURBING MIRACLE

Not long after Elisha witnessed his friend and mentor Elijah being taken to heaven, he was walking the road to Bethel when a fairly large group of youths began taunting him with chants of "Get out of here, baldy! Get out of here, baldy!" (see 2 Kings 2:23).

That doesn't sound like that bad of an insult to most people—especially those of us who are, shall we say, follically challenged. But Elisha wasn't amused.

Elisha could have just ignored the kids and went on his way. Or maybe made a mental note to contact the folks at Hair Club for Men. Instead, he turned to the youths and pronounced a curse on them in the name of the Lord. Just then, two bears came out of the woods and mauled forty-two of them.

At best, this seems like a strange response for such a trifling insult. At worst, it is very disturbing to know that forty-two boys met their end that day.

There just has to be more to this story than meets the eye—right?

Some scholars have suggested that this confrontation between the lads and Elisha was more than just some simple ribbing over his lack of hair, that these kids may have been an organized "gang" with bad intentions toward Elisha. This theory holds that their use of the phrase, "Go up" (KJV) referred to Elijah "going up" to heaven. The implication is that they wanted Elisha gone, as in dead.

There's no doubt that these young boys had shown disrespect to an elder, something that wasn't tolerated in the culture of that place and time. But there's another important principle here: these kids had spoken disrespectfully—even threateningly—to God's prophet, and the Lord wasn't about to stand for that.

Sure, they look mellow now. . .but don't make them mad!

LEADERS GO CRAZY

SCRIPTURES REFERENCED:
1 SAMUEL 21:10—15; 1 SAMUEL 16:18—19; 1 SAMUEL 17; 1 SAMUEL 18:6—9; DANIEL 4

Though modern governments make some crazy decisions, you can't assume that individual public officials are insane. Well, okay—maybe some of them.

But had you lived in Old Testament times, you'd have had plenty of reason to question the rightmindedness of two great leaders: David and Nebuchadnezzar.

CRAZY—OR WILY?

For a short time, David went crazy—like a fox. Running for his life from King Saul, David got into a tight spot in the city of Gath, where he put on a convincing display of kookiness to save his own skin.

The entire scenario began with a little song. David was a good-looking young dude who earned national fame by felling Goliath, the humongous warrior of the Philistines. When his slung stone found its way deep into Goliath's forehead, David became a hero—and the women of Israel began singing,

> *Saul has slain his thousands, and David his tens of thousands.*

If it's truly "the thought that counts," Saul should have appreciated being mentioned in the song. But something about rating only a tenth of that young punk David stuck in Saul's craw—and he began to watch David with increasing jealousy. The ill feeling soon progressed to attempted homicide, and David fled.

WELCOME TO PHILISTINE COUNTRY

The fugitive's path took him to Philistine lands and ultimately to Goliath's own hometown of Gath. Though David's incursion into enemy territory bought him a measure of safety from Saul, he soon heard strains of that song again—when servants of Gath's king, Achish, reminded their leader of David's fame. "Isn't this David, the king of the land?" they asked. "Isn't he the one they sing about in their dances:

> "*Saul has slain his thousands, and David his tens of thousands*'?"

"Gimme a *D*! Gimme an *A*! Gimme a *V*! . . ." Sometimes a little fame can be a dangerous thing, as David certainly found out.

That recognition spooked David, who decided his best way out was to seem, well, way out. So whenever King Achish and his men were nearby, the great warrior, poet, and man of God scratched on the doors and drooled all over his own beard.

King Achish, apparently subscribing to the "it's hard to soar with eagles when you work with turkeys" philosophy, scolded his servants for bringing

David feigned madness and escaped King Achish. King Saul—who actually had been driven mad by jealousy— wasn't so lucky. This nineteenth- century painting depicts Saul's death in battle with the Philistines.

TIMELINE OF DAVID'S LIFE

- Early (1 Samuel 16:1–23; 17:15)—Samuel anoints David king; harpist for King Saul
- From Bethlehem to Elah to Gibeah (1 Samuel 17:26–58)—David slays Goliath
- Between Gibeah and Jerusalem (1 Samuel 18:1–19:10)—Given a high rank in Saul's army; Saul is jealous of David and twice attempts to kill him
- From Gibeah to Ramah to Naioth to Gibeah (1 Samuel 19:18–21:42)—David flees to Samuel the prophet at Ramah; when he returns to Gibeah, Saul's son Jonathan alerts him of Saul's plan to kill David
- From Gibeah to Nob to Gath (1 Samuel 21:1–15)—Ahimelek gives David consecrated bread and the sword of Goliath; David feigns insanity in Gath
- From Gath to Adullam to Mizpah to the Forest of Hereth to Keilah (1 Samuel 22:1–5)—Removed his parents from danger in Mizpah; fought the Philistines in Keilah
- From Keilah to the Desert of Ziph to the Desert of Moan to En Gedi to the Desert of Moan (1 Samuel 21:14–24:22)—Formed a lasting allegiance with Jonathan in Ziph; spares Saul's life in En Gedi
- From the Desert of Maon to Carmel (1 Samuel 25–26)—Meets and marries Abigail, Nabal's widow; again spares Saul's life
- From the Desert of Maon and Carmel to Gath to Ziklag to Gath (1 Samuel 27:1–9)—Conquers Geshurites, Girzites, and Amelekites

David to him. "Am I so short of madmen that you have to bring this fellow here to carry on like this in front of me?"

With that dismissal, David split—and in his very right mind continued to elude the murderous Saul until the king later died in battle with those same Philistines.

- From Gath to Aphek to Ziklag to the south (1 Samuel 29:9–30:26)—Finds Ziklag ravaged by the Amalekites; travels south to recover the property of the people of Ziklag; returns to Ziklag
- From Ziklag to Hebron (2 Samuel 5:1–3)—Anointed king of Israel following the death of Saul and Jonathan
- From Hebron to Jerusalem to Baal Perazim to Jerusalem (2 Samuel 3:1–5:21)—Drives Philistines out of Baal Perazim and returns to Jerusalem
- From Jerusalem to Rephaim (2 Samuel 5:22–25)—Drives Philistines from Rephaim to Geba and Gezer
- From Jerusalem to Baalah to Gibeah (2 Samuel 6:2–11)—Went to bring the ark of the covenant back to Jerusalem, but it is left on Nakon's threshing floor
- From Jerusalem to the house of Obed-Edom (2 Samuel 6:14–23)—Brings the ark back to Jerusalem
- From Jerusalem to Metheg Ammah to Moab to Zobah to the Valley of Salt (2 Samuel 8:1–13)—Places Moab under his control; conquers Hadadezer in Zobah; kills eighteen thousand Edomites at the Valley of Salt
- From Jerusalem Helam (2 Samuel 10:17–19)—Conquers the Arameans
- Jerusalem (2 Samuel 11)—Sin with Bathsheba
- From Jerusalem to Rabbah (2 Samuel 12:29–31)—Inhabitants of Rabbah are treated with cruelty
- From Jerusalem to Mahanaim (2 Samuel 15–17)—Flees to Mahanaim following his son Absalom's coup; returns to Jerusalem and resumes the throne after Absalom's death
- From Jerusalem to Jabesh Gilead (2 Samuel 21:12–14)—Returns bones of Saul and Jonathan back to the land of Benjamin for burial in their father's tomb
- From Jerusalem for final battle with Philistines (2 Samuel 21:15–22)—Place of battle unknown
- Jerusalem (1 Kings 2:1–11)—David instructs his son and successor Solomon

CERTIFIABLY NUTS

There was nothing pretend about the insanity of King Nebuchadnezzar, the Babylonian leader in the time of the prophet Daniel. Overnight, ol' Neb was changed from the rich and powerful ruler of the world's mightiest kingdom to an unmanicured human cow having a bad hair day. (Confused? Don't worry—we'll explain.)

Nebuchadnezzar's mental episode began not with a song, but a dream. Lying in his kingly bed one night, the Babylonian big guy saw a giant tree stretching into the sky, producing plenty of fruit and sheltering both birds and beasts. Then the pleasant dream morphed into a nightmare: A messenger from heaven appeared, shouting, "Cut down the tree and trim off its branches; strip off its leaves and scatter its fruit. Let the animals flee from under it and the birds from its branches." The tree's stump and roots would remain, bound with iron and bronze rings; they would drip with dew and be surrounded by wild animals.

As he'd done before, Nebuchadnezzar dialed up his local dream interpreter, Daniel, who didn't like what he heard. "My lord," he cried, "if only the dream applied to your enemies and its meaning to your adversaries!"

The strange mental movie, Daniel said, meant that Nebuchadnezzar—the tree— would be driven away from human company to live among beasts, eating grass like a cow and soaking up the dew each morning. The only good news in the dream was that stump-and-roots thing—which meant King Neb would be restored to his position after seven "times," possibly meaning years.

In his own mind, Nebuchadnezzar's stature put even these giant redwoods to shame. But you know what comes after pride: destruction. The tree in Nebuchadnezzar's dream was chopped down and chopped up—a clear indication of trouble ahead for the king.

HERE IT COMES. . .

Twelve months later, as Nebuchadnezzar walked on the roof of his palace, a prideful thought touched off a spark that blew the king's world to pieces. "Is not this the great Babylon I have built as the royal residence, by my mighty power and for the glory of my majesty?"

Oops.

According to Daniel's report, "the words were on his lips" when a voice from heaven pronounced judgment on Nebuchadnezzar—a judgment that exactly paralleled the king's dream of a year before. Why? The pagan Babylonian needed to acknowledge the sovereignty of the one true God.

Without delay, Nebby's punishment went into effect. He was driven away from his human companions and began eating grass like a cow. The morning dews drenched his body, which underwent a *Twilight Zone*-style change: "His hair grew like the feathers of an eagle and his nails like the claws of a bird."

William Blake's late eighteenth-century painting captures the craziness of Nebuchadnezzar after God humbled the king for his pride. It's not a pretty picture.

A HAPPY ENDING

At the appointed time, Nebuchadnezzar turned his attention to heaven—to the God he had overlooked—and, in his words, "my sanity was restored." Not only his sanity, but his kingdom, authority, and splendor, too. In response, Nebuchadnezzar wrote an account of his experience for "the nations and peoples of every language, who live in all the earth," telling of God's mighty wonders.

Nothing crazy about that.

PREACHER DELIVERS KILLER SERMON

SCRIPTURES REFERENCED:

ACTS 20:7–12; 2 CORINTHIANS 10:10

There's an old joke about a little boy, bored and fidgeting through a church service, who noticed a row of small American flags lining the back of the sanctuary. Curious, he whispered to his mother, "What are those flags for?"

His mother whispered back, "It's Memorial Day weekend, Johnnie. Those flags are for all the boys who died in the service."

Johnnie was horrified. "Which one—morning or evening?"

IT'S NO JOKE

A biblical man named Eutychus might not have found that joke very funny. He *did* die in the service—the *church* service. Here's how it happened:

The apostle Paul was preaching in a city called Troas located in modern-day Turkey. With plans to head out of town the next day, Paul was giving the Troasites (Troasians? Okay, "people of Troas") their money's worth, talking on and on until midnight. And, let's face it—Paul didn't have a reputation as the world's most exhilarating speaker. The great missionary even admitted that in a letter to the church in Corinth, when he fed back the feedback he was getting: "His letters are weighty and forceful, but in person he is unimpressive and his speaking amounts to nothing."

For Eutychus, apparently, the dull speaker and the late hour were strikes one and two. A very warm room may have been strike three. Paul spoke in an upstairs meeting place (heat rises, you know) lined with lamps (putting off more heat) and filled with people (all generating about 98.6 degrees' worth of additional heat). We don't know exactly how many people were there, but the room was apparently crowded enough that Eutychus had taken a spot on a windowsill. Bad idea.

The young man progressed from blinking and yawning, to nodding off, to a sound sleep—at which point gravity took over. Eutychus fell out the window, three full stories to his death. Talk about a killer sermon.

IS THERE AN APOSTLE IN THE HOUSE?

Fortunately for Mr. E and his family and friends, that dull speaker was also a miracle-working apostle. Paul tramped down the steps to the lifeless body of Eutychus, threw his arms around the dead man, and shouted to the crowd, "Don't be alarmed. . . . He's alive!"

With that little speed bump smoothed over, Paul returned to the room and continued preaching—until daybreak.

BIBLICAL CHARACTERS RAISED FROM THE DEAD

Saying "My child, get up!", Jesus raises the twelve-year-old daughter of Jairus from the dead. Mourners who had moments before laughed at Jesus' comment, "She is not dead but asleep," are now astonished. The stained glass window is in Stanford University's Memorial Church.

- By Elijah: the son of the Zarephath widow (1 Kings 17:17–22)
- By Elisha: the son of the Shunammite woman (2 Kings 4:32–35)
- By Elisha: a man is raised when his body touches Elisha's bones (2 Kings 13:20–21)
- By Jesus: the son of the widow of Nain (Luke 7:11–15)
- By Jesus: the daughter of Jairus, a synagogue ruler (Luke 8:41–42, 49–55)
- By Jesus: Lazarus, the brother of Mary and Martha of Bethany (John 11:1–44)
- Upon the death and resurrection of Jesus: many saints rose from the dead (Matthew 27:50–53)
- By God the Father: Jesus Christ (Matthew 28:5–8; Mark 16:6; Luke 24:5–6)
- By Peter: a seamstress named Tabitha, or Dorcas (Acts 9:36–41)
- By Paul: a young man named Eutychus (Acts 20:9–10)

THE APOSTLE PAUL'S THIRD MISSIONARY JOURNEY

The miracle at Troas occurred during the apostle Paul's third missionary journey (see Acts 18:23–21:16), which took place c. AD 53–58. Paul traveled with the young preacher named Timothy during this journey. Here is their itinerary:

- Phrygia and Galatia (18:23)
- Ephesus (19)——Stays for two and one-half years; workers riot; writes 1 Corinthians and possibly Galatians
- Macedonia and Greece (20:1–2)—Writes 2 Corinthians
- Troas (20:6–12)—Stays for seven days, preaches long sermon; raises Eutychus from the dead
- Assos (20:13–14)—Aristotle taught here
- Ephesus (20:17–35)— Farewell speech to Ephesian elders
- Tyre (21:1–4)—Stays seven days
- Ptolemais (21:7)—Stays one day
- Caesarea (21:8–14)—Stays with Philip the evangelist
- Return to Jerusalem (21:15–18)

The amphitheater at Ephesus as it appears today. In the apostle Paul's time, this venue was the scene of a near-riot stirred up by silversmiths who made figurines of the goddess Diana. They complained that Paul's preaching was defaming the goddess—and, by the way, interfering with their business (see Acts 19:21–41).

JESUS' DEATH

SCRIPTURES REFERENCED:
COLOSSIANS 1:13–17; LUKE 19:40; MATTHEW 27:50–56; MARK 15:33–41; LUKE 23:44–49

Jesus' death is a marvel of the highest order. How can anyone really understand the sacrifice God made for His rebellious creation? We'll tackle the spiritual implications of Jesus' death elsewhere in this book, but for now, there are plenty of intriguing *physical* aspects of that dark day at Calvary.

THE EARTH SOBS

When Jesus died on the cross, it was almost as if the earth itself broke down with emotion.

That's no exaggeration of anthropomorphism. The apostle Paul once wrote of Jesus, "All things have been created through him and for him. . .and in him all things hold together." Those created things quietly honor God, even as humans, who should know better, often forget to. Once, in reply to Pharisees who wanted Jesus' followers to stop shouting so loudly in praise, the Lord said, "If they keep quiet, the stones will cry out." (Maybe it's time to retire that old insult, "Dumb as a box of rocks.")

As Jesus "gave up his spirit," the rocks and soil He had made and then walked on for some thirty-three years went into a convulsion of sorrow: Jerusalem and its vicinity were jarred by an earthquake that actually split rocks apart. The upheaval took place in the dark, because, in another example of creature grief, the sun had stopped shining at midday.

We are used to solar eclipses when the moon passes in front of the sun. It's an awesome sight, but the sun still shines behind the moon. Imagine how much more impressive it would be if the sun simply went out for a few hours—then started shining again!

Gospel writers Matthew, Mark, and John all identified Golgotha—a Hebrew name meaning "place of the skull"—as the place Jesus was crucified. This pockmarked hill, with caves looking something like the cavities of a skull—is believed by some to be the hill described in scripture.

GOLGOTHA: THE PLACE JESUS GAVE EVERYTHING

Golgotha is a place on the outskirts of Jerusalem where, after His arrest, trail, and condemnation to die, Jesus was crucified.

Golgotha is mentioned by all the Gospel writers except Luke, who calls it by the Latin name, Calvary. Scripture tells us Golgotha was beyond the walls of the city: "Jesus also suffered outside the city gate" (Hebrews 13:12). John adds that there was a garden there, and an unused tomb in which He was buried (John 19:41–42).

It was here that Jesus, spoke to a penitent criminal who was also suffering and dying on a cross, "Verily I say unto thee, Today shalt thou be with me in paradise" (Luke 23:43 KJV), where He made sure His mother, Mary, would be cared for, and where He made the sacrifice needed to bring humankind back into fellowship with God.

THAT'S INCREDIBLE!

Other amazing happenings accompanied Jesus' death. At the very moment Jesus breathed His last, "the curtain of the temple was torn in two from top to bottom," as if split by a divine karate chop. What was once a private place of meeting between God and the high priest was now open for everyone— through Jesus, the barrier between God and humans had been smashed.

And then there were the resurrections. Of course, Jesus' death was followed three days later by His own resurrection, and God promises that all who believe in Jesus will one day be raised to eternal life. But when Jesus died on Calvary, "the tombs broke open. The bodies of many holy people who had died were raised to life. They came out of the tombs after Jesus' resurrection and went into the holy city and appeared to many people."

Pretty shocking stuff—as is the fact that, out of the four Gospel writers, only Matthew felt compelled to note this particular miracle.

BIGGER AND BETTER

Don't get hung up on these physical miracles, impressive as they are. The real story of Calvary is the utterly breathtaking idea that God sent His only Son to die on a cross, to take the punishment for our sins. Want to know more? Read "Man Lives Forever" on page 274.

OH, THE PRECIOUS BLOOD OF JESUS. . .

The Bible teaches that it was Jesus shedding His blood on the cross that paid the penalty for our sins. According to the New Testament, Jesus' blood:

- Bought us (Acts 20:28)
- Atoned for our sins (Romans 3:25)
- Justified us (Romans 5:9)
- Redeemed us and provided forgiveness for our sins (Ephesians 1:7)
- Brought us near to God (Ephesians 2:13)
- Brings us to peace with God (Colossians 1:20)
- Obtained our eternal redemption (Hebrews 9:12)
- Cleansed our consciences (Hebrews 9:14)
- Gives us confidence to enter into the presence of God (Hebrews 10:19)
- Sanctifies us (Hebrews 10:29)
- Makes us holy (Hebrews 13:12)
- Redeemed us from an empty way of life (1 Peter 1:18–19)
- Purifies us from all sin (1 John 1:7)
- Freed us from our sins (Revelation 1:5)

Jesus' blood trickles out of wounds created by the crown of thorns. The sixteenth-century painting is by Niccolò Frangipane.

ROCK-STAR HAIR

SCRIPTURES REFERENCED:

2 SAMUEL 3:2–3; 2 SAMUEL 13–18; 1 KINGS 1:6; 1 SAMUEL 16:1–13

Had the concept of "celebrity" existed in Old Testament times, Absalom certainly would have been a paparazzi favorite. The drop-dead gorgeous, third-born son of Israel's king David was the Tom Cruise or Brad Pitt of his day.

TROUBLE IN PARADISE

Absalom was "all that"—and a bag of chips. "In all Israel there was not a man so highly praised for his handsome appearance as Absalom," the author of the Bible's second book of Samuel wrote. "From the top of his head to the sole of his foot there was no blemish in him."

Well, outwardly at least. Seems Absalom had some less-than-beautiful inner characteristics that were masked by the prettiness of his surface. A conniving brain lay inside his handsome head, which was topped off by a gorgeous mane of hair—one that Absalom allowed to grow and grow. Long before the "big-hair bands" of the 1980s, Absalom was tending a 'do he cut only when it got too heavy for his neck. The tipping point was the two-hundred shekel mark—about the weight of a five-pound bag of sugar in our world.

Speaking of that granular white stuff, sugar (and spice and everything nice) was not what Absalom was made of. More like power and pride and revenge on the side.

WE PUT THE "FUN" IN DYSFUNCTIONAL

Now, don't blame Absalom for all of his problems. Like a modern-day psychologist, we can trace many of his problems back to his father.

- *Cause #1:* Daddy liked women so much that he married at least six. Absalom grew up in a rather untraditional home, with half brothers and half sisters from a half dozen moms.
- *Cause #2:* Daddy could be indulgent at times. It was said of Absalom's next brother, Adonijah, that David "had never rebuked with him by asking, 'Why do you behave as you do?'"
- *Cause #3:* Daddy got mad about, but rarely dealt with, problems in his family—like the time his son Amnon raped his own half sister Tamar.

The great painter and sculptor Michelangelo created a famed statue of David as a fit, muscular young man. Throughout his lifetime, David was virile enough to sire almost twenty children.

DAVID'S OFFSPRING

First Chronicles 3:1–3 lists nineteen (that's not a misprint—19!) of David's sons by name and also reports that David had many other sons by his concubines as well as a daughter named Tamar (it's likely there were many other daughters). Here is a list of David's sons named in the Bible:

- Amnon, by Ahinoam from Jezreel
- Daniel, by Abigail from Carmel
- Absalom, by Maakah, daughter of King Talmai of Geshur
- Adonijah, by Haggith
- Shephatiah, by of Abital
- Ithream, by Eglah
- Shammua, by Bathsheba
- Shobab, by Bathsheba
- Nathan, by Bathsheba
- Solomon, by Bathsheba
- Ibhar
- Elishua
- Eliphelet
- Nogah
- Nepheg
- Japhia
- Elishama
- Eliada
- Eliphelet

If David couldn't deal with that last situation, Absalom, who was a full brother to Tamar, certainly would.

FRATRICIDE AND REBELLION

Absalom stewed for two years over the violation of Tamar, then found his chance to exact revenge during a sheep-shearing festival. The pretty boy waited until the rapist got happily drunk, then ordered his men to strike down Amnon. At that point, Absalom split, running away some eighty miles north to his grandfather's place in Geshur.

David mourned not only the death of Amnon but the disappearance of Absalom. The king "longed to go to Absalom," unaware that his beautiful son would soon be plotting to take over the country.

In time, Absalom returned to Israel—and, with a perfect politician's touch, began working the crowds. When unhappy people were bringing complaints to the king, Mr. Suave would stop them on the way, hear out their gripes, and tell them, "Look, your claims are valid and proper, but there is no representative of the king to hear you. . . . If only I were appointed judge in the land! Then everyone who has a complaint or case could come to me and I would see that they receive justice."

People ate that up, and they loved it even more when Absalom turned the rules of personal engagement on their head. As the king's son, Absalom could expect people to bow down before him. But whenever they did, he would reach out

Teddy Roosevelt campaigns for president in 1912. Almost three thousand years earlier, Absalom also stumped for the hearts of his countrymen—against his own father, David.

to them, pull them up, and kiss them. According to the author of 2 Samuel, Absalom "stole the hearts of the people of Israel."

Before long, Absalom was turning those hearts against his own father, setting himself up as king in the town of Hebron. When David heard that, he knew there was trouble—and he ran.

WASN'T THIS STORY ABOUT HAIR?

Oh, yes. And Absalom's rock-star hair will factor into the next, and final, scene in his life.

Ultimately, "King" Absalom's followers geared up for battle with those men who'd remained loyal to David. In a fierce battle in a heavy forest, some twenty thousand men were killed or injured—but the one man whose particular story we know is Absalom's.

"He was riding his mule," the Bible records, "and as the mule went under the thick branches of a large oak, Absalom's hair got caught in the tree. He was left hanging in midair, while the mule he was riding kept on going."

With his gorgeous hair thus snarled, Absalom was a sitting (or, should we say, "suspended") duck. He was killed by David's military commander, Joab, who plunged three javelins into his heart, and ten other soldiers who struck at him with their own weapons.

Absalom's body was dumped into a pit and covered with a large pile of rocks. So ended the career of "Israel's sexiest man," whose stunning good looks benefited him very little.

Maybe things could have been different had Dad passed along a key truth from his own early years. At the time the prophet Samuel anointed David the future king of Israel, God had passed over David's older, bigger, and perhaps handsomer brothers. Why? "The LORD does not look at the things people look at. People look at the outward appearance, but the LORD looks at the heart."

It was truly a "bad hair day" for Absalom when his gorgeous locks got caught in tree branch. Soon, he'll have a chest full of spears.

TOUGH PUNISHMENTS

SCRIPTURES REFERENCED:
PROVERBS 23:13–14; LEVITICUS 24:10–23; NUMBERS 15:32–36; DEUTERONOMY 21:18–21; 1 CORINTHIANS 5:6

Spanking has gotten a bad rap in recent years. But there was a time, not that terribly long ago, when a good swift swat (or several) were the discipline *du jour* of parents, teachers, and principals.

Those who denounce corporal punishment today should thank God they didn't live in Old Testament times.

This well-used paddle is in an Italian museum of education—and today's students are probably glad it's only for display.

POW, BIFF, SOCKO

Solomon believed the physical pain of a spanking would lead to eternal spiritual benefits for a troublemaking kid, and he immortalized the idea in a proverb: "Do not withhold discipline from a child. . . . Punish them with the rod and save them from death." You have to wonder how many spankings Solomon himself may have administered, considering the size of his family (see "Man Marries 700 Women" on page 26). After a while, it seems his arm would have fallen off.

The arm of discipline risked soreness on many occasions, especially if heavy rocks were involved. Stoning was also a commonly prescribed punishment for a variety of misdeeds. And stoning, in case the concept is unfamiliar to you, was designed to result in *death*.

Here's a sampler of stonable offenses, each from the Israelites' time of wilderness wandering:

- *Blasphemy:* When a young man, in the heat of a fistfight, uttered a curse against God, onlookers took him to Moses, who got the official judgment from God Himself: "Take the blasphemer outside the camp. All those who heard him are to lay their hands on his head, and the entire assembly is to stone him."
- *Breaking the Sabbath:* When a man was found gathering firewood on the Sabbath, the Israelites' official day of rest, onlookers (again) took him to Moses, who got the official judgment (again) from God Himself: "The man must die. The whole assembly must stone him outside the camp."
- *Being Rebellious:* Moving preemptively, God didn't wait for an example of youthful rebellion, but passed down a law as a warning—and what a frightful warning it was: "If someone has a stubborn and rebellious son who does not obey his father and mother and will not listen to them when they discipline him," God told Moses, "his father and mother shall take hold of him and bring him to the elders at the gate of his town. They shall say to the elders, 'This son of ours is stubborn and rebellious. He will not obey us. He is a glutton and a drunkard.' Then all of the men of his town shall stone him to death."

CRUEL AND UNUSUAL?

In our "more enlightened" time, when we try to "understand" troublemakers and criminals, biblical punishments may seem a little over the top. But God had His reasons for cracking down hard.

Knowing that a little evil goes a long way (the author's paraphrase of the apostle Paul's comment, "a little yeast leavens the whole batch of dough"), God wanted His people to nip problems in the bud, to prevent them from spreading and growing into much larger issues. Six times in the rules He passed down in the book of Deuteronomy, God commanded, "You must purge the evil from among you."

And harsh punishments had the added benefit of deterrence. When God ruled that rebellious sons should be stoned, he told Moses, "All Israel will hear of it and be afraid."

No doubt. And spankings don't seem so tough in comparison.

"Children are a heritage from the Lord, offspring a reward from him."
Psalm 127:3

THE BIBLICAL TAKE ON CHILDREN/PARENTING

- Genesis 18:19—Parents should raise their children in the ways of the Lord.
- Proverbs 22:6—Giving a child good training in the ways of God increases the odds that he or she will live godly lives as adults.
- Colossians 3:21, Ephesians 6:4—Fathers should discipline their children, but should be careful not to provoke them or exasperate them.
- Proverbs 13:24—Disciplining children is not easy, but it is a demonstration of love to do so.
- Proverbs 23:13—Discipline can help keep a child in the faith and teach him or her right from wrong.
- Proverbs 29:15—Failing to discipline your children could mean later heartache and shame, while consistent discipline will help instill godly wisdom.
- Proverbs 29:17—A child who is properly disciplined will bring great joy to his or her parents.

- Psalm 139:13—16—Children are a gift from the God who lovingly designs them and gives them their personalities and physical traits.
- Deuteronomy 4:9—God wants parents to pass on to their children the wisdom they have learned living lives of faith in Him.
- Deuteronomy 6:6—9—Godly parents should be diligent to pass along to their children a love for God's Word. They should provide constant reminders of reading, knowing, and living according to the scriptures.
- Isaiah 38:19—Children should be able to see in their parents a love for God and an appreciation for His goodness and faithfulness.
- 2 Timothy 1:5—Parents who live sincere lives of faith have a good chance of passing that faith on to their children.
- 2 Timothy 3:14—15—Children need to learn the principles of the Christian faith from a very early age.

SAINTS 3, LIONS 0

SCRIPTURES REFERENCED:

1 SAMUEL 17:34–37; JUDGES 14:1–7; DANIEL 6

Sure, it sounds like a low-scoring football game between New Orleans and Detroit. But even though you can find baseball in the Bible (Genesis 1:1—"In the big inning. . ."), gridiron references are in short supply. No, these Saints were real human beings (in the biblical sense of "people set apart to God"), the Lions real beasts, and the final result a real rout.

WHEN MEN ROAR

The lion is called the "King of the Jungle," having been voted "Most Likely to Eat Us All" in high school. But the great cat didn't stand a chance against two familiar Bible men.

- *Cat Fight #1:* Shepherd boy David, volunteering for action against the Philistine war machine Goliath, tells King Saul that he can take the heat of the battle's kitchen. "When a lion or a bear came and carried off a sheep from the flock, I went after it, struck it and rescued the sheep from its mouth," David reported. "When it turned on me, I seized it by its hair, struck it and killed it. Your servant has killed both the lion and the bear; this uncircumcised Philistine will be like one of them." To prove his words were more than hot air, David promptly went out and felled the giant tree of a man.

We can only wonder what Samson's girlfriend thought of his new cologne—Eau de Lion. See next page. . .

- *Cat Fight #2:* Israelite judge Samson (see "The Bible's *Terminator*" on page 42), on a stroll to see his girlfriend, is pounced upon by a young lion near the town of Timnah. Bad move, kitty. Samson responds to the sneak attack with overwhelming force: "He tore the lion apart with his bare hands as he might have torn a young goat." Having barely broken a sweat, Samson continued into town to visit his gal.

IS THAT YOUR STOMACH GROWLING?

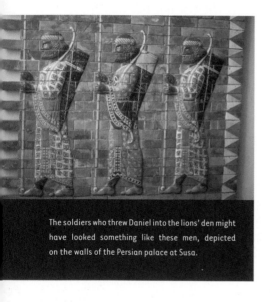

The soldiers who threw Daniel into the lions' den might have looked something like these men, depicted on the walls of the Persian palace at Susa.

Then there's the story of Daniel. He never whipped a lion into submission, because he didn't have to. The fearsome felines became pussycats in Daniel's presence.

If you've ever been to Sunday school, you've heard the story: The exiled Jew Daniel rises to prominence in Persia, causing jealousy among homegrown officials who trick King Darius into passing a stupid law. The new rule demands that everyone pray only to the king for the next thirty days—violators will be prosecuted, and those found guilty "shall be thrown into the lions' den."

Unfazed, Daniel did what Daniel always did. He opened his window toward Jerusalem, got on his knees, and prayed—not to Darius, but to God. His enemies, thinking they'd won, tattled to the king, who very reluctantly upheld his law. Daniel descended into the den.

Oddly, the lions passed on this tasty morsel, allowing Daniel to live through the night before he was pulled back out of the pit the next morning. It wasn't that the creatures weren't hungry: When Darius ordered the jealous officials to be thrown into the den, "the lions overpowered them and crushed all their bones."

A LITTLE HELP HERE

So why would this powerful king of the beasts seem so helpless around mere men? Samson, we know, was a pretty tough dude, but David was just a kid tending sheep. Daniel was probably around ninety—and unlikely to daunt lions with his physical presence.

Any discussion of Bible marvels must take into account the miracle-working power of the Bible's Author. In Samson's case, "the Spirit of the Lord came powerfully upon him" as he ripped the lion to pieces. David said it was "the Lord who rescued me from the paw of the lion and the paw of the bear." Daniel also credited God, who "sent his angel, and he shut the mouths of the lions."

These lion tamers knew where their success started. Without God, they would have been wise to follow the advice of those television stunt shows: "Don't try this yourself!"

SOME BIBLICAL PRAYER TRIVIA

The Bible's first mention of prayer: "Seth also had a son, and he named him Enosh. At that time people began to call on the name of the Lord" (Genesis 4:26).

- The King James Bible's first use of the word *pray* (in reference to speaking to God): "My Lord, if now I have found favour in thy sight, pass not away, I pray thee, from thy servant" (Genesis 18:3).

- The King James Bible's first use of the word *prayer*: "For thou, O Lord of hosts, God of Israel, hast revealed to thy servant, saying, I will build thee an house: therefore hath thy servant found in his heart to pray this prayer unto thee" (2 Samuel 7:27).

- The Bible's last use of the word *prayer*: "The smoke of the incense, together with the *prayer*s of God's people, went up before God from the angel's hand" (Revelation 8:4).

- Number of verses that include the word *prayer*: 128 (KJV), 154 (NIV)

- Number of prayers in the Bible: approximately 650

- Number of answered prayers in the Bible: approximately 450

GOAT DISH OFF THE MENU

SCRIPTURES REFERENCED:
GENESIS 9:1–3; LEVITICUS 11:1–23; EXODUS 23:19; EXODUS 34:26; DEUTERONOMY 14:21; ISAIAH 66:13; MATTHEW 23:37

Though the very first humans, Adam and Eve, were vegetarians, meat eaters can trace their lineage all the way back to Noah. It was he who, shortly after the great flood, received God's new culinary dispensation: "Everything that lives and moves will be food for you. Just as I gave you the green plants, I now give you everything."

SOME RESTRICTIONS APPLY

Later rules would limit the menu somewhat—"clean" animals (like the cow, sheep, or quail) were in, "unclean" animals (like the camel, pig, and rabbit) were out.

The goat was "in," though one particular recipe was decidedly "out." Three times in the Old Testament, God told His people not to cook a young goat in its mother's milk.

Why? God didn't say—He just inserted that prohibition into lists of various dos and don'ts for the Israelites. But perhaps we can guess at His reasoning: Mothers provide love, protection, and nourishment for their children. Using a mother's milk to boil her child turns the whole concept of motherhood on its head—and might reflect poorly on God, who occasionally compared Himself to a mother. "As a mother comforts her child, so will I comfort you," He said through the prophet Isaiah. "Jerusalem, Jerusalem," Jesus lamented, "how often I have longed to gather your children together, as a hen gathers her chicks under her wings."

Whatever the reason may be, baby goat boiled in its mother's milk is not an acceptable dish. Order steak instead.

PASS THE GRASSHOPPERS!

We live in a time when we can go to a fine restaurant and order up some "surf 'n' turf" for dinner—also known as a steak and lobster. But did you know that during Old Testament times, only half of that meal was considered "clean"—meaning God allowed you to eat it? Cud-chewing animals with divided hooves (cattle, for example) were clean, but lobsters were not, meaning they were not to be eaten.

On the other hand, animals with divided hooves that do not chew cud (pigs, for example) were out. So no pork chops or ham or bacon. Also on the "not to be eaten list" were animals such as camels, rock badgers, and rabbits.

Anything that lived in the water and had fins and scales (also known as fish) were considered clean and could be eaten, but not other animals that live in the water (shellfish, crustaceans, and the like).

It probably wouldn't have disappointed you to know that moles, rats, and mice (rodents) were not to be eaten, nor were any species of lizard (who would want to eat those anyway?). Bats were out, as were birds of prey (eagles, vultures, buzzards, hawks, and owls), crows, ostriches, seagulls, pelicans, storks, herons, and hoopoes (whatever *those* are).

On the other hand, if you wanted to get your daily ration of protein, a good place to get it would be a heaping helping of locusts, grasshoppers, and crickets. Those bugs were considered clean and could be eaten, but other winged insects were out.

Yes	No	Yes	No	Yes	No

PREACHER GETS STONED

SCRIPTURES REFERENCED:

2 CORINTHIANS 11:16–29; EPHESIANS 5:18; ACTS 14:8–20; ACTS 7:54–8:1; ACTS 9:1–19; COLOSSIANS 1:24

In modern usage, the word *stoned* generally means "drunk" or "on drugs." So it would be at least a tad scandalous to hear of a preacher getting stoned.

"Once was I stoned," the apostle Paul wrote to the church at Corinth (KJV), a few years before telling the Christians in Ephesus, "Do not get drunk on wine, which leads to debauchery. Instead, be filled with the Spirit." So, what's the deal? Was Paul one of those "do as I say not as I do" kind of preachers?

Hardly.

OUCH!

When Paul got stoned, it was literal. In Bible times, *stoned* meant, well, "stoned"—hit with rocks, smashed to a bloody pulp. It's not a pretty picture, but it was a common punishment for a variety of offenses (see "Tough Punishments on page 170).

In Paul's case, it happened like this: At the city of Lystra in Asia Minor (modern-day Turkey), Paul and his fellow missionary Barnabas healed a man crippled from birth. When the townspeople learned what had happened, they decided Paul and Barnabas were gods—and tried to offer sacrifices to them. Of course, the two men would have none of that, telling the crowd, "We too are only human, like you. We are bringing you good news, telling you to turn from these worthless things to the living God."

The awe of the miraculous healing was soon forgotten, though. Riffraff from Antioch and Iconium, the last two towns Paul and Barnabas had visited, appeared in Lystra to stir up trouble for the preachers they hated. And

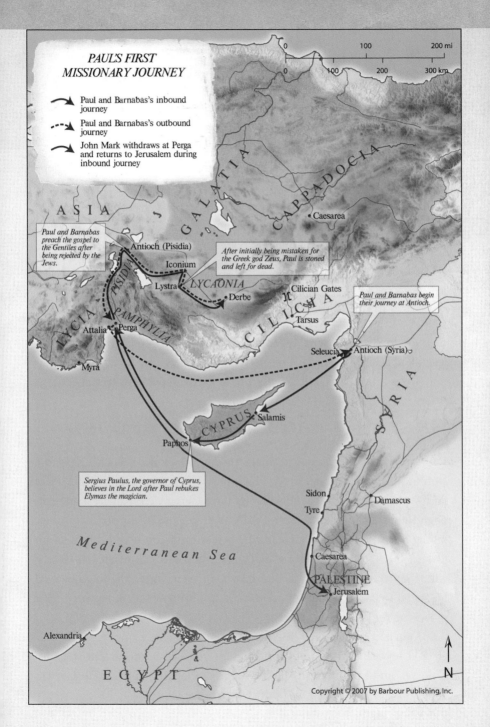

PAUL'S FIRST MISSIONARY JOURNEY

Paul and Barnabas's inbound journey

Paul and Barnabas's outbound journey

John Mark withdraws at Perga and returns to Jerusalem during inbound journey

Paul and Barnabas preach the gospel to the Gentiles after being rejected by the Jews.

After initially being mistaken for the Greek god Zeus, Paul is stoned and left for dead.

Paul and Barnabas begin their journey at Antioch.

Sergius Paulus, the governor of Cyprus, believes in the Lord after Paul rebukes Elymas the magician.

Copyright © 2007 by Barbour Publishing, Inc.

This propaganda painting, commissioned by England's King Henry VIII, shows the Gospel writers Matthew, Mark, Luke, and John stoning the pope. Whatever Henry's purpose in displaying the image, the painting is 180 degrees out of phase. Jesus' disciples would have been much more likely to be on the receiving end of any stonings!

they convinced the people of Lystra that the "gods" they had so recently wanted to worship were actually men worthy of stoning.

Barnabas apparently slipped out of the crowd's grasp, but Paul was caught, stoned, dragged out of the city, and left for dead. But like the Energizer bunny, Paul revived and went back into Lystra. The next day, he and Barnabas continued their missionary journey to the city of Derbe.

If stoning seems an extreme punishment for telling people about Jesus, Paul said it was all part of the job. He even boasted that his hardships proved he was a true servant of Christ: "I have worked much harder, been in prison more frequently, been flogged more severely, and been exposed to death again and again. Five times I received from the Jews the forty lashes minus one. Three times I was beaten with rods, once I was pelted with stones. . . ."

WHAT GOES AROUND COMES AROUND

Interestingly, the first time we meet Paul in the Bible, he's a witness to a stoning. Known at that time as Saul, he was no friend of the Christian faith—and served as a coat-check boy for the angry crowd that made Stephen the first Christian martyr. Saul was there, and he "approved of their killing him." Soon, Saul had started a career of violence and intimidation toward Jesus' followers that ended only when Jesus Himself had a chat with the troublemaker on a road near Damascus. Soon, having changed his name to Paul, the former persecutor was himself being persecuted for preaching the message of Christ.

So Paul had come full circle. The stoner had become a stonee, and he was glad: "I rejoice in what I am suffering for you," he wrote to Christians in Colosse, "and I fill up in my flesh what is still lacking in regard to Christ's afflictions, for the sake of his body, which is the church."

Nothing scandalous about that.

This statue of the apostle Paul stands in front of St. Peter's Basilica in Rome. Paul is shown holding a sword, a reference to his description of the Bible as "the sword of the Spirit" (Ephesians 6:17)—and also a hint to the way he died. Tradition says he was beheaded.

THE LIFE OF THE APOSTLE PAUL

- Born in Tarsus (Acts 9:11)
- A Pharisee himself and son of a Pharisee (Acts 23:6)
- Studied under the Jewish teacher Gamaliel (Acts 22:3)
- Citizen of Rome (Acts 22:25–28)
- Sister lived in Jerusalem (Acts 23:16)
- Chief persecutor of the early church (Acts 9:1–3; 22:4)
- Present at the stoning of Stephen (Acts 7:58)
- Converted near Damascus (Acts 9:3–18)

- First missionary journey, with Barnabas (Acts 13–14)
- Second missionary journey, with Silas (Acts 15:36–18:22)
- Third missionary journey, with Timothy (Acts 18:23–28:31)
- In Jerusalem (Acts 21:17–23:15)
- In Caesarea (Acts 24:10–26:29)
- Taken to Rome (Acts 27:14–28:10)
- Arrival at Rome (Acts 28:16)
- Preaches in Rome (Acts 28:30–31)
- Paul's final words (2 Timothy 4:6–8)

DÉJÀ VU AT THE WATER'S EDGE

SCRIPTURES REFERENCED:
EXODUS 14; NUMBERS 11:28; JOSHUA 3–4; 2 KINGS 2; HEBREWS 13:5

Déjà vu is that sense of having seen something before—a familiarity of experience that the Bible's Moses, Joshua, Elijah, and Elisha could well have shared.

THE GREAT DIVIDE

It's a classic story, one that even Hollywood horned in on: Moses, leading the Israelites out of their slavery in Egypt, raises his staff and parts the Red Sea. The water miraculously divides, the people walk through on dry ground, and the pursuing Egyptian soldiers are wiped out when the waters rush back together.

Having served as Moses' aide since his youth, Joshua undoubtedly walked between those walls of water himself. Years later, with Moses dead and Joshua leading the Israelites to the Promised Land, the former right-hand man oversaw a similar marvel at the water's edge.

NO BOATS REQUIRED

The Jordan River was all that stood between God's people and Canaan, the land they'd spent forty years trying to reach. On the night before the crossing, Joshua teased the people with the slightest hint of the next day's miracle: "Consecrate yourselves, for tomorrow the LORD will do amazing things among you."

Without the ark of the covenant's miraculous powers, modern Israeli soldiers must use a portable bridge to cross rivers.

Amazing, indeed. When Joshua sent the priests carrying the ark of the covenant forward, they marched right into the Jordan, flowing high in its annual flood stage. But when the priests' feet touched the moving liquid, "the water from upstream stopped flowing. It piled up in a heap a great distance away, at a town called Adam in the vicinity of Zarethan, while the water flowing down to the Sea of the Arabah (that is, the Dead Sea) was completely cut off."

As in Moses' day, the Israelites crossed on dry ground that had been inundated only moments before. The priests who carried the ark lingered in the middle of the river until everyone passed, then walked out themselves— at which point the Jordan came rushing back into its place. This time, however, there were no pursuing enemies to be washed away.

LET'S DO IT AGAIN

In the days of Elijah and Elisha, the Jordan River divided twice—and in quick succession. On the day Elijah changed his address from earth to heaven (see "Men Escape Death—Permanently" on page 124), the two prophets were walking along the Jordan when Elijah whacked the water with his cloak. According to the Bible's second book of Kings, "The water divided to the right and to the left, and the two of them crossed over on dry ground."

Moments later, Elijah's bus arrived in the form of flaming horses and a chariot of fire. Whisked away from Elisha's presence, Elijah's cloak fluttered to the ground behind him; when Elisha picked it up and smacked the Jordan again, "it divided to the right and to the left, and he crossed over."

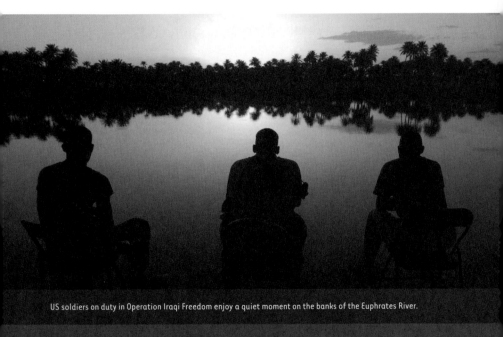

US soldiers on duty in Operation Iraqi Freedom enjoy a quiet moment on the banks of the Euphrates River.

IMPORTANT BIBLICAL RIVERS

- **Euphrates**—A river that Genesis 2:14 describes as flowing out of Eden's river. The Euphrates River flows from Turkey to the Persian Gulf and is one of the rivers that enclose Mesopotamia. God covenanted with Abram that the land from the river of Egypt, on Judah's southwestern border, to the Euphrates would be given to his descendants (Genesis 15:18). The Lord renewed the promise with Joshua as Israel entered the Promised Land (Joshua 1:4). In the book of Revelation John describes the vial of wrath that will be poured out on the Euphrates, drying it up (Revelation 16:12).
- **Gihon**—A spring near Jerusalem where Solomon was anointed king by Zadok the priest, at King David's command (1 Kings 1:33–34). King Hezekiah, threatened by war with Babylon, cut a shaft that redirected the water of this spring directly into Jerusalem (2 Chronicles 32:30).
- **Jabbok**—This river flows into the Jordan River from the mountains of Gilead. Jacob met the Lord near here, at Peniel, after he sent his family across the ford of Jabbok (Genesis

DEVOTIONAL THOUGHT FOR THE DAY

God's really good at parting water. But one thing He'll never part with is *us*.

"God has said," wrote the author of Hebrews, "'Never will I leave you; never will I forsake you.' "

Just think about that the next time you see a river or lake!

32:22). When the Amorite King Sihon refused to let Israel pass through his land on their way to the Promised Land, Israel conquered his land, north to the Jabbok (Numbers 21:21–25).

- **Jordan—** A river flowing from Palestine's Lake Huleh, south to the Sea of Galilee and on to the Dead Sea; the Jordan River defined the eastern edge of Canaan. On its way toward Canaan, Israel conquered lands east of the Jordan River, including the eastern part of the Amorite holdings. Following the conquest of the Promised Land, most of Israel's land lay west of the Jordan. John the Baptist performed many baptisms in the Jordan River, including the baptism of Jesus (Matthew 3:6, 13–17).
- **Kebar—**The prophet Ezekiel was near this Mesopotamian river, with other exiles to Babylon, when he saw a prophetic vision of God and His cherubim (Ezekiel 1:1).
- **Kerith—**A ravine east of the Jordan River, in Gilead. After the prophet Elijah foretold a drought that would last for a few years, God sent him to Kerith, where he could hide from King Ahab of Israel. Here Elijah was fed by ravens and drank from the brook in the ravine (1 Kings 17:3–5).
- **Kidron—**A brook and valley just east of Jerusalem, between Jerusalem and the Mount of Olives, that David passed over when he left Jerusalem to keep his rebellious son Absalom from destroying the city (2 Samuel 15:23). Kings Asa and Josiah burned idols near the Kidron Brook. Josiah also burned former kings' pagan altars there. Jeremiah predicted that when Jerusalem was rebuilt, this area would be holy to the Lord (Jeremiah 31:40).
- **Kishon—**A river in the middle of Palestine, running from Mount Gilboa north to the Mediterranean Sea. Sisera gathered his army from Harosheth to this river, where he engaged in battle with Barak and his troops. Barak and Deborah's song tells us that the river swept some of the warriors away (Judges 4–5). At this brook, after his confrontation with the prophets of Baal on Mount Carmel, the prophet Elijah killed the pagan prophets (1 Kings 18:40).
- **Nile—**The name "Nile River" doesn't appear in the King James Bible, but newer Bible translations mention the Nile River as the stream where Pharaoh's daughter found the baby Moses floating in a basket (Exodus 2:3–5) and as the site of the ten plagues (Exodus 7:15, 20). In these passages, the King James refers to it as "the river."
- **Ulai—**A river (or canal) near Susa, in the Elam province. Here Daniel had his vision of the ram and the goat, which symbolized the Median, Persian, and Greek empires (Daniel 8:2, 16).

666, AGAIN, AGAIN, AGAIN

SCRIPTURES REFERENCED:
REVELATION 13:1–18; 1 KINGS 10–11; LUKE 16:13

Most everyone can agree there's something creepy about the number 666. Horror-movie writers and heavy-metal bands have splashed the triple-six over their celluloid, vinyl, and digital recordings in hopes of creating some shock here and there. (Isn't it ironic that the figure originates in scripture?)

THE BIBLE'S 666S

The number is mentioned once in the book of Revelation, in connection with a future "beast, coming out of the earth." Sporting a pair of lamblike horns, the creature speaks "like a dragon"—and forces human beings of the last days to worship a companion beast from the sea. Both beasts possess a really nasty streak—making war, calling down fire from heaven, and killing all who object to beast worship. And this beast from the earth leaves his mark on people—literally. The beast's number, 666, will be imprinted on the right hand or forehead of every person who wants to buy or sell in the end times.

But that's not the only time the number 666 appears in the Bible. Another occurrence is in the story of Solomon, king of Israel, well-known for his wisdom, his wealth, and his womanizing (see "Man Marries 700 Women" on page 26). The figure applied most directly to the second *w* of Solomon— his wealth—but may also have factored into the third.

"The love of money is a root of all kinds of evil," the Bible says (1 Timothy 6:10), though money itself is just a tool for the exchange of goods and services. Gold has been recognized as a medium of exchange since almost the dawn of human history: As far back as Genesis 2:11, which describes the rivers flowing through the Garden of Eden, scripture mentions "the land of Havilah, where there is gold."

A seventeenth-century artist's conception of the interior of Solomon's temple in Jerusalem

SOLOMON'S GREAT ACCOMPLISHMENTS

Solomon, son of King David, reigned as the kingdom of Israel's third king for forty years. During that time, he earned respect throughout the ancient world for the great things he accomplished during his time in power. During his reign, he not only oversaw the rise of the kingdom of Israel to its highest place ever. He also:

- Oversaw the construction of the first temple in Jerusalem, a place that would be a center of worship for the next four hundred years
- Constructed his royal palace in central Jerusalem, near the temple
- Constructed a system that supplied water for the entire city
- Fortified the city of Jerusalem, helping to protect it from its enemies
- Strengthened or rebuilt the cities of Hazor, Megiddo, and Gezer
- Rebuilt several major cities and ports in the region

Solomon is also believed to have built Tadmor, an important city in the center of Syria.

According to the Bible's first book of Kings, Solomon amassed gargantuan amounts of money. Ships would travel the known world, filling up on gold to bring back to the king's collection—to the tune of 666 talents each year. Scholars believe that in Old Testament times, a talent was a unit of measure equal to about seventy-five pounds. If that's true, Solomon would have acquired about twenty-five tons of gold each year, worth over a billion dollars in our time, when gold sells for a premium price of more than a thousand dollars an ounce.

What would Solomon do with his 666 talents of gold each year? For one thing, he outfitted his palace with plenty of gold accents: large and small shields (five hundred in all), an elaborate throne, goblets, and "all the household articles in the Palace of the Forest of Lebanon were pure gold."

Of course, with seven hundred wives and three hundred concubines populating the palace, Solomon *needed* plenty of gold articles to go around. Feeding, clothing, and buying birthday presents for that massive harem certainly cost a bit of coin, too.

ANY CONNECTION?

So a question arises: What relationship might there be between the 666 of Revelation and the 666 of Solomon? Are the numbers simply coincidental, or could there be a deeper connection?

In Revelation, the goal of the beast is to separate people from God. Gold—or more generally, money—can easily accomplish the same thing, as Jesus once noted: "No one can serve two masters. Either you will hate the one and love the other, or you will be devoted to the one and despise the other. You cannot serve both God and money." That's even truer when the money is coupled with sex.

Solomon ultimately crashed and burned when he let his wives lead him into idol worship. And that brings our story full circle: Solomon's 666 ends like Revelation's.

THE REIGN OF SOLOMON, AND THE REST OF THE EARLY HISTORY OF ISRAEL

Included in the Bible are twelve books called "history books." You can read about King Solomon, as well as many other amazing people in these books:

- Joshua—The Israelites capture and settle the Promised Land of Canaan.
- Judges—Israel goes through cycles of sin, suffering, and salvation.
- Ruth—Loyal daughter-in-law pictures God's faithfulness, love, and care.
- 1 Samuel—Israel's twelve tribes unite under a king.
- 2 Samuel—David becomes Israel's greatest king—but with major flaws.
- 1 Kings—Israel divides into rival northern and southern nations.
- 2 Kings—Both Jewish nations are destroyed for their disobedience to God.
- 1 Chronicles—King David's reign is detailed and analyzed.
- 2 Chronicles—The history of Israel, from Solomon, through division, to destruction.
- Ezra—Spiritual renewal begins after the Jews return from exile.
- Nehemiah—Returning Jewish exiles rebuild the broken walls of Jerusalem.
- Esther—Beautiful Jewish girl becomes queen, saves fellow Jews from slaughter.

Jerusalem, where much of Bible history occurred, is dominated today by the gold-topped Dome of the Rock, a Muslim shrine. It's constructed above the site of the temple that Solomon built.

PRIEST URGES DIVORCE!

SCRIPTURES REFERENCED:
MALACHI 2:16; EZRA 7:1–10; DANIEL 2:46–49; EZRA 7:11–26; DEUTERONOMY 7:1–3;
EZRA 9–10

hate divorce," God once said through His prophet Malachi. So why did a priest named Ezra urge his fellow Jews to send their wives and children packing?

WHO IS THIS GUY?

Regardless of his rather shocking suggestion, Ezra boasted some pretty impressive credentials. A direct descendant of the very first high priest, Aaron, Ezra was "a teacher well versed in the Law of Moses, which the LORD, the God of Israel, had given." God had blessed Ezra because he not only *studied* the Word of God, he *obeyed* it, as well.

Ezra lived in Babylon, once the capital of the mighty Babylonian Empire, now under the control of Persia. Many Jews had been taken captive when Babylon overran Jerusalem about 150 years earlier, and some of the really sharp ones had worked for the Babylonian kings (as Daniel had for Nebuchadnezzar). About eighty years before Ezra, Persia conquered the Babylonians and treated the Jews more humanely. Now Ezra and the current king, Artaxerxes, were on good terms.

Good terms, indeed. When Ezra asked to travel to Jerusalem to beautify the temple and restore Jewish worship there, he got what he wanted—along with a letter from the king that promised, among other things:

- silver and gold from the king's treasury;
- permission to resume sacrifices on the altar of the Jerusalem temple;

- authority to appoint magistrates and judges for the Jews;
- power to order punishment—up to and including the death penalty—for those who broke God's laws.

Artaxerxes, however, forbade one thing. In a truly historical ruling, the king told Ezra that *no taxes* would be permitted on the people traveling to Jerusalem with him.

EXILES RETURN TO JUDEA

The extent of the Persian Empire at the time of Ezra (c. 458 BC)

➤ Judean exiles return under Zerubbabel's leadership

➤ Judean exiles return under Ezra's leadership

Ezra leads the exiles along a shorter, more dangerous route without military escort.

AN APPALLING DISCOVERY

Ezra's journey went smoothly, and the band of returning exiles celebrated its arrival in Jerusalem with tons of sacrifices—literally. They offered to God twelve bulls, ninety-six rams, seventy-seven male lambs, and twelve male goats. But, like the smoke rising off the altar, the warm, fuzzy feelings were soon to dissipate.

SOME THINGS TO KNOW ABOUT EZRA

- He was the son or grandson of Seraiah.
- He was a direct descendant of Aaron, the brother of Moses.
- The name *Ezra* is a shortened form of Azariah, which means "Yahweh has helped."
- Ezra was well-versed in the law and was a scribe and teacher.
- Because the hand of God was upon Ezra, the Persian king Artaxerxes gave him everything he wanted.
- Ezra led 1,496 men (as well as many more women and children) from Babylon back to Jerusalem, a journey that took 119 days.
- Ezra fasted and prayed before the journey, asking God to keep them safe. They arrived safely back in Jerusalem with all the treasure Artaxerxes had allowed them to take intact.
- Ezra devoted himself to the study of the law.
- Ezra had been in Jerusalem for four and a half months when he became aware of the problem of intermarriage among the Jewish people. When he found out, he displayed his grief by tearing his clothes, pulling out his hair, and repeatedly throwing himself down to the ground. When the people saw his response, they trembled in fear.
- Eventually, the people agreed to separate themselves from foreign wives (and their resulting children). The separations were complete within three months.
- Tradition holds that Ezra recorded the books of 1 Chronicles, 2 Chronicles, Ezra, and Nehemiah. It is also possible that he wrote the book of Esther.

The new arrivals quickly noticed something strange about their fellow Jews already living in Jerusalem, descendants of those who had rebuilt the city and its temple several decades before: The old-timers had married indiscriminately, taking spouses from groups like the Canaanites, Hittites, Perizzites, Jebusites, Ammonites, Moabites, and Amorites. All those "ites" had been off-limits for centuries, since God had originally warned the Hebrews through Moses against intermarriage.

When somebody told Ezra, he was shocked—so upset that he tore his own clothes, then ripped hair out of his head and beard. (Ouch!) And then he prayed:

I am too ashamed and disgraced, my God, to lift up my face to you, because our sins are higher than our heads and our guilt has reached to the heavens. . . . We have forsaken the commands you gave through your servants the prophets when you said: "The land you are entering to possess is a land polluted by the corruption of its peoples. By their detestable practices they have filled it with their impurity from one end to the other. Therefore, do not give your daughters in marriage to their sons or take their daughters for your sons."

A figurine of the Canaanite god Baal, from about a thousand years before Ezra. God had commanded the Israelites not to marry Canaanites (or several other people groups) in the Promised Land, because their of their false religion. Ezra found that that ancient command had been ignored.

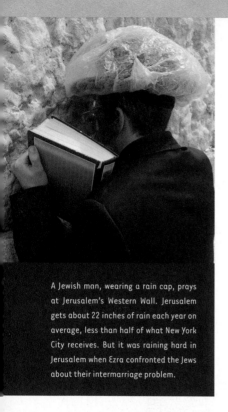

A Jewish man, wearing a rain cap, prays at Jerusalem's Western Wall. Jerusalem gets about 22 inches of rain each year on average, less than half of what New York City receives. But it was raining hard in Jerusalem when Ezra confronted the Jews about their intermarriage problem.

WHAT TO DO?

One of the guilty actually proposed the remedy for the problem. A man named Shecaniah approached Ezra to say, "We have been unfaithful to our God by marrying foreign women. . . . Now let us make a covenant before our God to send away all these women and their children. . . . Let it be done according to the Law."

Surprise must have shown on Ezra's face, because Shecaniah pressed the matter further. "Rise up; this matter is in your hands," he told the priest. "We will support you, so take courage and do it."

After a time of fasting and praying, Ezra called all of the exiles to gather in Jerusalem. They did, sorry about the sin they committed—and sorry to be standing outside in a rainstorm.

When Ezra called the crowd to confess and part ways with their foreign wives, they agreed almost unanimously: "You are right! We must do as you say." Only four men—Jonathan, Jahzeiah, Meshullam, and Shabbethai—resisted.

Over the next three months, officials sorted out who was guilty of intermarriage. The final count: 111 Jewish men had transgressed God's law and needed to say good-bye to their wives and families.

TOUGH STUFF

That's awful, you may be thinking. And it is.

But so was the idolatry that had plagued Israel for centuries, idolatry often instigated and encouraged by the foreigners among the Israelites.

Ultimately, Ezra's bitter pill cured the patient. The forced divorces mark a turning point in Jewish history, as idol worship seemed to pass from the scene in Israel.

EZRA'S PRAYER OF CONFESSION OF HIS PEOPLE'S SINS

O my God, I am ashamed and blush to lift up my face to thee, my God: for our iniquities are increased over our head, and our trespass is grown up unto the heavens.

Since the days of our fathers have we been in a great trespass unto this day; and for our iniquities have we, our kings, and our priests, been delivered into the hand of the kings of the lands, to the sword, to captivity, and to a spoil, and to confusion of face, as it is this day.

And now for a little space grace hath been shewed from the LORD our God, to leave us a remnant to escape, and to give us a nail in his holy place, that our God may lighten our eyes, and give us a little reviving in our bondage.

For we were bondmen; yet our God hath not forsaken us in our bondage, but hath extended mercy unto us in the sight of the kings of Persia, to give us a reviving, to set up the house of our God, and to repair the desolations thereof, and to give us a wall in Judah and in Jerusalem.

And now, O our God, what shall we say after this? for we have forsaken thy commandments, Which thou hast commanded by thy servants the prophets, saying, The land, unto which ye go to possess it, is an unclean land with the filthiness of the people of the lands, with their abominations, which have filled it from one end to another with their uncleanness.

Now therefore give not your daughters unto their sons, neither take their daughters unto your sons, nor seek their peace or their wealth for ever: that ye may be strong, and eat the good of the land, and leave it for an inheritance to your children for ever.

And after all that is come upon us for our evil deeds, and for our great trespass, seeing that thou our God hast punished us less than our iniquities deserve, and hast given us such deliverance as this; Should we again break thy commandments, and join in affinity with the people of these abominations? wouldest not thou be angry with us till thou hadst consumed us, so that there should be no remnant nor escaping?

O LORD God of Israel, thou art righteous: for we remain yet escaped, as it is this day: behold, we are before thee in our trespasses: for we cannot stand before thee because of this.

EZRA 9:6–15 KJV

WATER CATCHES FIRE!

SCRIPTURES REFERENCED:

1 KINGS 18:16–40; ISAIAH 8:1–4; HOSEA 1:1–3; EZEKIEL 1, 4, 37

There's a reason firefighters use so much water in their business—it works. Water—good old H$_2$0—smothers, quenches, and extinguishes fires. If you're trying to build a fire, you'll keep the water as far away from the flames as possible. And you'll want to start with dry matches, dry paper, and dry wood. It would be crazy to do anything else.

So what was the prophet Elijah doing pouring water over the raw materials of his "burnt offering"?

THOSE WACKY PROPHETS

Prophets could be a tad strange, you know:

- There was Isaiah, who hung one of the longest names imaginable on his son: Maher-Shalal-Hash-Baz. Meaning "quick to the plunder, swift to the spoil," it was a symbolic message of a coming Assyrian invasion.
- There was Hosea, whose symbolic messages to Israel involved marrying a rather unsavory woman (see "Prophet Marries a Prostitute!" on page 224).
- And then there was Ezekiel, who saw visions of flying saucers and animated skeletons (see "UFO Files" on page 246), and who once lay on his side for more than a year to symbolize an upcoming siege of Jerusalem.

Elijah's actions were anything but symbolic. Dousing the wood and the bull of his sacrifice was an action intended not to carry a subtle, mystical message, but rather to beat observers over the head with an example of God's power.

AND IN THIS CORNER. . .

A kind of metaphysical boxing match pitted the all-time, undefeated (and undefeatable) champion God against a brassy challenger named Baal. Elijah played the role of fight promoter, setting up a "ring" on Mount Carmel for the big event.

Why? Israel's king, Ahab, had turned completely away from God. With his evil foreign wife, Jezebel, egging him on, Ahab now supported the worship of the false god, Baal, believed by many to hold lightning in his hand. Elijah knew it was time for a showdown.

"Summon the people from all over Israel to meet me on Mount Carmel," the prophet commanded the king. "And bring the four hundred and fifty prophets of Baal and the four hundred prophets of Asherah, who eat at Jezebel's table."

Ahab did as he was told, proving that God's representatives still held a certain sway over their idol-worshipping rulers. With more than eight hundred false prophets and an unnumbered crowd of straying Israelites gathered at the mountain, Elijah got down to business. "How long will you waver between two opinions?" he shouted. "If the LORD is God, follow him; but if Baal is God, follow him."

A figurine of Asherah, on display in an Israeli museum.

Unmoved by Elijah's challenge, the people kept silent. But they began to murmur, "What you say is good," when Elijah threw down the gauntlet: "Get two bulls for us. Let Baal's prophets choose one for themselves, and let them cut it into pieces and put it on the wood but not set fire to it. I will prepare the other bull and put it on the wood but not set fire to it. Then you call on the name of your god, and I will call on the name of the LORD. The god who answers by fire"—Baal's supposed specialty—"he is God."

ROUND ONE. . .DING!

If the crowd was expecting fireworks, they would be disappointed—for a while, at least. Baal's prophets called out to their "god" all morning, without so much as a peep in reply. Switching from audio to visual, the false prophets started to dance around their altar. Still no Baal.

"Shout louder!" Elijah urged his opponents. With just a touch of sarcasm, Elijah suggested that Baal was deep in thought, busy with something more important, or perhaps even traveling. Worse yet for those who prefer a 24/7 kind of god, Elijah theorized, "Maybe he is sleeping and must be awakened."

TWO KINGS VERSUS A PROPHET OF GOD

Elijah ministered in Israel during the reigns of two evil kings—one of which was among the worst ever to hold the throne.

Ahab (c. 874–853 BC) did great evil in the sight of God. He married Jezebel, daughter of the king of Zidon, and began worshipping the pagan "god" Baal. Because of that, God sent Israel a drought that only the prophet Elijah could break. Ahab was killed in a battle with Syria.

Ahaziah (c. 853–852 BC), the son of Ahab reigned for two years and walked in the pagan ways of his parents. When he fell through a lattice in his chamber and was badly hurt, he sought help from the pagan god Baal-zebub. God sent Elijah to the king's messenger, asking if there was no God in Israel. Twice Ahaziah sent soldiers to Elijah, to demand that he come to the king. Twice Elijah called fire down on them. When a third captain came more humbly, Elijah went to the king and prophesied that he would die.

Drummers perform in worship to the Hindu god of war and victory, Murugan. In Elijah's day, the prophets of Baal shouted, danced, and ultimately slashed themselves in hopes of attracting their god's attention.

Desperate times, they say, call for desperate measures, so the prophets of Baal grabbed their swords and spears. It wasn't preparation for an attack on Elijah, but another attempt to get Baal's attention. Slashing at themselves, "as was their custom," the 450 prophets of Baal actually bled for the cause. But even that was for naught. Evening came, and Baal was still quieter than a mouse—with laryngitis.

ROUND TWO. . .DING! DING!

Putting a halt to the embarrassing scene at Baal's altar, Elijah called the people to the altar of the Lord. It was in sorry shape due to decades of neglect, so Elijah built a new one out of twelve stones, one for each of the tribes of Israel. Then he dug a trench around the altar, put the firewood on top, and placed the dismembered bull on the wood. And, oh, yeah—remember that business about pouring water on a sacrifice? This is the time; this is the place.

"Fill four large jars with water and pour it on the offering and on the wood," Elijah instructed the crowd.

They did.

"Do it again," Elijah ordered.

They did.

"Do it a third time," Elijah commanded.

They did.

The word "waterlogged" well describes the meat and wood of Elijah's offering at this point. After twelve large jars of water, the altar was soaked—and the trench around it had become a moat. And those fireworks the people had been expecting? Here comes the man to light the fuse. . . .

Today, cable cars transport visitors to the top of Mount Carmel. In Elijah's day, they traveled on foot—probably carrying all of the elements for the big showdown between God and Baal.

IT'S A KNOCKOUT

In human terms, Elijah faced 450 to 1 odds against the prophets of Baal. In spiritual terms, with the one true God on his side, Elijah was unbeatable.

With the preparations for the sacrifice complete, the prophet paused for a moment to offer a prayer. "LORD, the God of Abraham, Isaac and Israel," Elijah intoned, "let it be known today that you are God in Israel and that I am your servant and have done all these things at your command."

Yeah, but what about the fireworks?

"Answer me, LORD, answer me," Elijah continued, "so these people will know that you, LORD, are God, and that you are turning their hearts back again."

This statue, on Israel's Mount Carmel, commemorates Elijah's victory over the prophets of Baal and Asherah.

And with that, all heaven broke loose.

God sent a blazing bolt from the blue that incinerated not only the wood and meat on the altar, but the stones comprising the altar and the soil on which they stood. The heavenly fire even surged through the water-filled trench, combusting the inert liquid like gasoline.

You want fireworks? You got 'em.

The thrilling scene was one of the last things Baal's prophets ever saw. At Elijah's command, they were promptly executed by the onlookers.

FIFTY-TWO MORE WORDS AND YOU'RE DONE

When even water burns, there's clearly something unusual going on. On Mount Carmel some twenty-eight hundred years ago, the natural order of things was turned on its head by the God who had created that natural order of things. His supernatural ability proved that He was (and *is*) the only true God.

WELCOME TO EMEROD CITY

SCRIPTURES REFERENCED:
1 KINGS 15:23–24; EXODUS 9:10; 2 CHRONICLES 21:18–19; ACTS 12:19–23; 1 SAMUEL
4–6; 2 SAMUEL 6:1–7

O dd maladies dot the pages of scripture. Consider these cringe-inducing examples:

- the undefined disease of the feet that apparently killed King Asa of Judah
- the boils that broke out through Egypt when Moses tossed some furnace soot into the air
- the incurable abdominal disease suffered by King Jehoram of Judah, whose "bowels came out. . .and he died in great pain"
- the flesh-eating worms that caused the demise of Judea's evil King Herod (see "What a Way to Go" on page 100).

Then there was the epidemic of tumors—*emerods*, in the King James Version—that struck the Philistine towns of Ashdod, Gath, and Ekron when they took turns housing the ark of God, stolen from the Israelites in battle. Medical details in a moment, but first the historical background.

WHO'S WHO

The time of Israel's "judges" was winding down (see "The Bible's *Terminator*" on page 42), but the nation had not yet gotten a king. So its main leaders were a prophet—Samuel—and an aging priest—Eli. Filling out the cast were Eli's two rotten-egg sons, Hophni and Phinehas, who were priests in name but not in behavior: they stole meat from the people's offerings to God and even slept with the women who served at the tabernacle.

The recklessness of Hophni and Phinehas led to their early deaths, punishment from a very angry God, who arranged for the two "priests"

ASHDOD, GATH, AND EKRON—PHILISTINE ROYALTY

Ashdod, Gath, and Ekron were three of the five royal cities of the Philistines—the other two being Gaza and Ashkelon (see Joshua 13:3).

Ashdod was located midway between Gaza and Joppa, three miles from the Mediterranean Sea. It was a center of worship for the Philistine god Dagon. The area had been granted to the tribe of Judah (Joshua 15:47), but the tribe never took possession of it. King Uzziah, one of the Bible's known Philistine fighters, took possession of it for Judah, but the Assyrians took it fifty years after his death.

Gath is known as a place that suffered calamity after the Philistines took the ark of the covenant (1 Samuel 6:17) and as the birthplace or residence of Goliath (1 Samuel 17:4). David, before he became king, fled to Achish, king of Gath (1 Samuel 21:10, 27:2–4). David later conquered Gath (2 Samuel 8:1).

Ekron was located about eleven miles north of Gath. Like Ashdod, it was also granted to the tribe of Judah and later to the tribe of Dan (Joshua 19:40–48) but was later taken by the Philistines (1 Samuel 5:10). Ekron was the last place to where the Philistines took the ark before they sent it back to Israel (1 Samuel 5:10; 6:1–8).

Modern Ashdod is an important industrial center, and the largest seaport in Israel. Its beaches are also popular with tourists.

to die in battle with the Philistines. Though you have to give the boys credit for doing their military duty, they took part in a really dumb stunt on the battlefield: helping bring the ark into the war zone as a kind of good-luck charm.

If it wasn't for bad luck, Hophni and Phinehas would have had no luck at all. They were slaughtered along with thirty thousand Israelite soldiers, and the ark was captured by Israel's archenemy. When news of the disaster reached the overweight, ninety-eight-year-old Eli, he fell backward off his chair, breaking his neck and dying, too.

MORE TRAUMA

The mayhem and death would continue—this time on the side of the Philistines.

Like a victorious hockey team celebrating the Stanley Cup, the Philistines carried the ark to the town of Ashdod, putting it inside the temple of their god, Dagon. With a long, hard day behind them, the Philistines all took hot bubble baths and went to bed—only to find the next morning that the statue of Dagon had fallen off its pedestal and was lying on its face in front of the ark. Apparently, God's delicious sense of irony was wasted on the Philistines, who set Dagon back on his pedestal and went on their way.

Dagon is often portrayed as half man, half fish. He was completely powerless in the presence of God's ark.

The next morning, Dagon was down again—this time broken in pieces. The people of Ashdod, meanwhile, started feeling unwell themselves, as God "afflicted them with tumors." It didn't take much to realize the ark was the source of their ailments, so they decided to ship it off to the nearby town of Gath.

Gee, thanks, the people of Gath must have thought, because God then struck the people of that city, "both young and old," with an outbreak of tumors, as well. In the immortal language of the King James Version, "they had emerods in their secret parts." Soon, Gath was sending the unwelcome wagon on to Ekron.

The bad news had traveled fast to Ekron, and people there met the ark at the city limits with cries of, "They have brought the ark of the god of Israel around to us to kill us and our people." The Ekronites wanted to dispatch the ark as quickly as possible—but couldn't do so quickly enough. "Those who did not die," the writer of 1 Samuel reported, "were afflicted with tumors, and the outcry of the city went up to heaven."

The rat was implicated in spreading the "Black Death," a plague that killed millions in Europe around 1350. When the Philistines of Bible times came down with a troublesome plague, they fashioned rats from gold and sent them to Israel, along with the ark of the covenant, as a guilt offering (1 Samuel 6).

WHAT IS IT, DOCTOR?

So what were these tumors, these mysterious emerods that caused such suffering?

A footnote in the Bible's New International Version offers a hint as to where the tumors appeared: "in the groin." That's according to the Septuagint, an ancient Greek translation of the Old Testament. *The New Strong's Expanded Dictionary of Words in the Hebrew Bible* explains that the word *emerod* comes from a root that means "to burn" and indicates an inflamed boil or ulcer. In the groin area, that could very well be *hemorrhoids*. (Say the two words together—what do you think?)

We'll resist any jokes about Preparation H, because this was a serious plague on the unwitting Philistines. And it showed once again how serious God was about people respecting Him and His ark. Remember Uzzah? He was an Israelite who once tried to steady the ark on its cart when the oxen pulling it stumbled, and God struck him dead for his "irreverent act."

God's justice can be pretty frightening—and it was excruciating for Jesus on the cross. We can all be thankful we live in an age of grace, don't you think?

PHYSICAL/MENTAL PROBLEMS MENTIONED IN THE BIBLE

Ague/wasting diseases (Leviticus 26:16)
Abscess/boils (2 Kings 20:7; Exodus 9:10)
Atrophy/shriveling (Job 16:8; 19:20)
Blindness (Job 29:15; Matthew 9:27)
Deafness (Psalm 38:13; Mark 7:32)
Dropsy/swelling (Luke 14:2)
Dumbness (Proverbs 31:8; Matthew 9:32)
Dysentery/incurable disease of the bowels (2 Chronicles 21:12-19; Acts 28:8)
Epilepsy/seizures (Matthew 4:24; 17:15)
Festering sores/scab (Deuteronomy 28:27)
Fever (Deuteronomy 28:22; Matthew 8:14)
Itch (Deuteronomy 28:27)
Inflammation/extreme burning (Deuteronomy 28:22)
Issue of blood (Matthew 9:20)
Lameness (2 Samuel 4:4; 2 Chronicles 16:12)
Leprosy (Leviticus 13:2; 2 Kings 5:1)
Loss of appetite (Job 33:20; Psalm 107:18)
Loss of strength (Psalm 102:23; Ezekiel 7:17)
Palsy/paralysis (Matthew 8:6; 9:2)
Plague (Numbers 11:33; 2 Samuel 24:15, 21, 25)
Speech impediment (Mark 7:32)
Sunstroke (2 Kings 4:18-20; Isaiah 49:10)
Tumors/hemorrhoids (Deuteronomy 28:27; 1 Samuel 5:6; 5:12)
Ulcers/emerods (Isaiah 1:6; Luke 16:20)
Wasting disease/consumption (Leviticus 26:16; Deuteronomy 28:22)
Worms (Acts 12:23)

People of Bible times didn't enjoy the medical advances of recent decades. But if Jesus, Elisha, Peter, or Paul were nearby, they didn't need them!

MAGICIANS MOCK MOSES' MIRACLES

SCRIPTURES REFERENCED:
GENESIS 41:41–43; GENESIS 47:11–12; EXODUS 1:8–14; EXODUS 7–12; JOB 38:4, 32; JOB 40:2

God's ten plagues on ancient Egypt constitute an entire group of Bible marvels. The fact that Egyptian magicians could duplicate some of the miracles is a bit of a Bible shocker.

A TALE OF TWO NATIONS

Egypt was the schoolyard bully, pushing around the weak and defenseless Israelites. The northern African nation had once lifted a Jewish slave-boy, Joseph, to second in command, then put out the welcome mat for his eleven brothers and their father, Jacob, during a famine in their homeland of Canaan. Now Egypt viewed the rapidly growing family as a potential rival. A new pharaoh, "to whom Joseph meant nothing," forced the Israelites into hard labor and even ordered their baby boys to be killed at birth.

Israel needed a champion, and God provided one in the form of a reluctant shepherd named Moses. Getting his marching orders from the burning bush

Put a baby in a basket. Then put the basket in the river. What happens next? The fact that the basket didn't sink may have been the first miracle associated with Moses.

(see "Look Who's Talking" on page 228), Moses, along with his older brother, Aaron, took God's demand to "Let my people go!" directly to the pharaoh—who was a tad slow in grasping the message. God would send ten miraculous plagues on Egypt before the king was finally convinced to let the Israelites scram.

MIRACLE, COUNTERMIRACLE

To establish his legitimacy with Egypt's big cheese, God told Moses that Aaron should perform a little warm-up miracle: "Say to Aaron," the Lord said, " 'Take your staff and throw it down before Pharaoh,' and it will become a snake."

That's exactly what happened—but then Pharaoh's "wise men and sorcerers" duplicated the feat by their own "secret arts." The sticks these men carried were tossed to the ground to morph into slithering serpents, too.

Plague number one—turning the waters of Egypt to blood—was soon to follow. Moses struck the Nile River with his staff, and Aaron lifted his stick over the rest of Egypt's waters—streams, canals, ponds, and reservoirs— and all the life-sustaining liquid in the entire nation turned a deadly red. Even the water in buckets and jars went bad, forcing the Egyptians to dig new wells to survive.

But guess what? Pharaoh's magicians were able to mimic this miracle, too. Then they did the same with the next plague.

One week after wrecking Egypt's water supply, God prompted Moses to threaten the nation with an amphibious invasion. " 'This is what the Lord says: Let my people go, so that they may worship me. If you refuse to let them go, I will send a plague of frogs on your whole country.'"

God to Pharaoh: "The Nile will teem with frogs. They will come up into your palace and your bedroom and onto your bed, into the houses of your officials and on your people, and into your ovens and kneading troughs. The frogs will come up on you and your people and all your officials" (Exodus 8:3–4). Pharaoh didn't listen.

God's message to Pharaoh—as well as to Job—was basically, "I'm more powerful, more knowledgeable, more everything than you are." His power over nature, throughout the entire universe, proves that!

Aaron knew the drill. He raised his staff over Egypt's sticky red rivers and ponds, and frogs began to materialize out of the water to the point that they "covered the land."

And, once again, Pharaoh's magicians did the same thing, making even more frogs appear in Egypt.

HEY, WAIT A MINUTE. . .

But Pharaoh surely didn't *want* more frogs. Nor had he needed his magic men to turn more water into blood.

Though it seemed like the wise men and sorcerers of Egypt were showing a power equal to God's, they were actually making Pharaoh's situation much worse. What the Big Guy needed was someone to purify the water and make the frogs disappear. *Just great*, Pharaoh must have grumbled when additional frogs flopped into his palace and onto his own bed. Even the magicians' staffs-become-snakes trick turned out to be bogus, since "Aaron's staff swallowed up their staffs."

The fact is that Pharaoh's sorcerers were completely overmatched by Moses, Aaron, and God. The Egyptian conjurers admitted as much when Aaron struck the dust of the ground with his staff, creating a swarm of gnats like the world had never seen before. Unable to duplicate this feat, the "wise men" said their first wise thing: "This is the finger of God." From that point on, Pharaoh's magicians let well enough alone.

TRIFLING WITH GOD

People like to think they have ultimate control over their own lives, or that they're pulling one over on God, or that He's not as powerful as the Bible says He is, or that [insert your favorite reasoning here]. But Egypt's wise men learned firsthand that God is not to be trifled with. His power goes so far beyond humankind's that it's silly even to consider a comparison.

"Where were you when I laid the earth's foundation?" God once asked Job. "Can you bring forth the constellations in their seasons? . . . Will the one who contends with the Almighty correct him?"

People may bluff, but God holds every card.

20 MIRACLES ASSOCIATED WITH MOSES

- Moses' staff turns into a serpent and back into a staff (Exodus 4:2–4)
- Moses' hand becomes leprous and then returns to normal (Exodus 4:7)
- Aaron's staff becomes a serpent and swallows up the sorcerers' serpents (Exodus 7:10–12)
- God hides the Hebrews with a cloud (Exodus 14:19–20)
- The Red Sea parts, the sea bottom made dry land (Exodus 14:21)
- The waters of the Red Sea return and drown the Egyptian army (Exodus 14:23–28)
- Bitter waters at Marah made sweet (Exodus 15:23–25)
- Hebrews fed with quail (Exodus 16:11–13)
- Hebrews fed with manna (Exodus 16:14–24)
- Moses strikes rock in Horeb to produce water for the Hebrews (Exodus 17:1–6)
- Fire from the Lord consumes burnt offering (Leviticus 9:22–24)
- Miriam made leprous and then healed (Numbers 12)
- Complaining Hebrews burned up by fire from the Lord until Moses intercedes (Numbers 11:1–2)
- Fire from the Lord consumes 250 men who offered incense (Numbers 16:16–18, 35)
- Earth opens up and swallowed Korah and his men (Numbers 16:28–33)
- Plague that kills 14,700 stopped by making an offering of incense (Numbers 16:46–50)
- Aaron's staff grows buds and blossoms (Numbers 17)
- Moses strikes rock twice to bring forth water (Numbers 20:1–11)
- Moses makes brass serpent and puts it on a pole. Those bitten by a fiery serpent live when they look at the serpent (Numbers 21:5–9)
- Moses appears on the Mount of Transfiguration with Jesus (Luke 9:28–36)

THAT OMNISCIENCE THING

SCRIPTURES REFERENCED:

PSALM 147:4; DANIEL 5; LUKE 12:1–7; JEREMIAH 31:34

One of the great adjectives we use to describe God—*omniscient*—isn't even found in the Bible. But the concept sure is.

OM-WHAT?

Our friends at Merriam-Webster define *omniscient* as "having infinite awareness, understanding, and insight; possessed of universal or complete knowledge." Sounds like a pretty good description of the Father in heaven.

Consider that God knows the exact number of stars in the universe. For metropolitan folk, who never see the stars over the glare of city lights, this example might lack impact. But if you've ever looked up on a cool, clear night in the country, you've probably seen a breath-taking display of stars—and good luck counting them. Not only does God *number* the stars, according to the psalm writer, He "calls them each by name."

It isn't just stars that God is keeping track of. A biblical king, Belshazzar, learned the hard way that God keeps tabs on world rulers, too. In the middle of a big beer bash (actually, a wine bash) Belshazzar was hosting, God Himself appeared unexpectedly. Well, kind of. A disembodied hand wrote a mysterious message on the wall, which could be read only by the old dream interpreter Daniel (see "Leaders Go Crazy" on page 150). The first word of the message, "mene," meant "God has numbered the days of your reign and brought it to an end." Belshazzar's end came that very night, by way of assassination.

IMPORTANT NAMES/TITLES OF GOD:

- Abba, Father (Mark 14:36)
- Ancient of Days (Daniel 7:9)
- Consuming Fire (Hebrews 12:28–29)
- Creator (Isaiah 40:28)
- Deliverer (Psalm 70:5)
- Dwelling Place (Psalm 90:1)
- Eternal God (Genesis 21:33)
- Father (Isaiah 64:8)
- Father of Our Lord Jesus Christ (Colossians 1:3)
- Fortified Tower (Proverbs 18:10)
- Fortress (Jeremiah 16:19)
- Glorious Crown (Isaiah 28:5)
- God Almighty (Genesis 17:1)
- God Most High (Genesis 14:18–19)
- God My Savior (Habakkuk 3:17–18)
- God of Abraham, Isaac, and Jacob (Exodus 3:15)
- God of All Comfort (2 Corinthians 1:3)
- God of All the Earth (Isaiah 54:5)
- God of Heaven (Nehemiah 1:4)
- God of Peace (Hebrews 13:20–21)
- Hiding Place (Psalm 32:7)
- Holy One (Isaiah 43:15)
- Horn of My Salvation (Psalm 18:2)
- I Am Who I Am (Exodus 3:14)
- Jah (Psalm 68:4 KJV)
- Jehovah (Exodus 6:3 KJV)
- Jehovahjireh, or the Lord Will Provide (Genesis 22:14)
- Jehovahnissi, or the Lord Is My Banner (Exodus 17:15)
- Jehovahshalom, or the Lord Is Peace (Judges 6:23–24)
- Judge (Psalm 75:7)
- Judge of All the Earth (Genesis 18:25)
- King (1 Samuel 12:12)
- King Eternal, Immortal, Invisible (1 Timothy 1:17)
- King of Glory (Psalm 24:7–10)
- Lawgiver (Isaiah 33:22)
- Light (Psalm 27:1)
- Living God (Daniel 6:20)
- Lord of Hosts (Zechariah 8:22 KJV)
- Lord Our Righteousness (Jeremiah 23:6 KJV)
- Lord Who Heals (Exodus 15:26)
- Majesty in Heaven (Hebrews 1:3)
- Potter (Isaiah 64:8)
- Redeemer (Isaiah 54:8)
- Refuge (Deuteronomy 33:27)
- Rock (1 Samuel 2:2)
- Savior (Isaiah 45:21)
- Shepherd (Psalm 23:1)
- Shield (Psalm 5:12)
- Spring of Living Water (Jeremiah 2:13)
- Strength (Exodus 15:2)

Whatever else God may be—and He is much more than we can ever imagine—He is a loving Father to all who come to Him through Jesus.

HE KNOWS YOU, TOO

Well, okay, you may be thinking, *stars and kings are big, important things— but what do they have to do with me?* So glad you asked!

Speaking to His twelve disciples and thousands of ordinary people following Him around, Jesus once said, "The very hairs of your head are all numbered." Now, don't think that's just a silly exercise God does to show off His omniscience—according to Jesus, that kind of attention from God should give people confidence.

God knows each tiny, inconsequential bird— how much more does He care about you?

"Don't be afraid," Jesus taught, because God even keeps track of the world's sparrows—small birds that sold then for less than a half penny each. The true point of Jesus' example? "You are worth more than many sparrows."

WHAT DOESN'T HE REMEMBER?

Omniscience means God knows everything about everything. But He actually chooses to *dis*-remember some things, a sort of conscious forgetfulness.

The prophet Jeremiah spoke of a time when people would know the Lord personally, when God would "forgive their wickedness and will remember their sins no more."

Thank God for that kind of forgetfulness!

In Christ, our transgressions will be washed from God's memory like this sandcastle in the waves.

Adoption: One of God's great promises in scripture.

SOME GREAT PROMISES OF SCRIPTURE

- Abundant life in Christ (John 10:10; 14:19; Romans 6:8, 11; Ephesians 2:1, 5–6; 1 John 5:12)
- Adoption into God's family through Christ (Romans 8:14–15; 9:26; 2 Corinthians 6:18; Galatians 4:4–7; 1 John 3:1–2)
- Confident access to God (Hebrews 10:19–20; Ephesians 2:18; 3:12; 1 John 5:14–16)
- Eternal life with God in heaven (John 14:2–3; Romans 2:7; 1 Corinthians 2:9; Hebrews 4:9; 1 Peter 9; 2 Peter 3:13; Revelation 3:4)
- Forgiveness of sin (Psalm 65:3; 103:9–12; Isaiah 43:25; 44:22; Micah 7:18–19; Matthew 26:28; Ephesians 1:7; Hebrews 8:2; 10:17; 1 John 1:9; Revelation 1:5)
- God's enduring love (Jeremiah 31:3; Zephaniah 3:17; John 16:27; Ephesians 2:4; 2 Thessalonians 2:16)
- God's mercy (Exodus 33:19; Deuteronomy 4:31; Psalm 103:13; Isaiah 30:18; 48:9)
- Justification through Jesus Christ (Acts 13:39; Romans 3:24; 2 Corinthians 5:21)
- No condemnation (Romans 8:1; 8:33–34)
- Reconciled to God through Christ (Romans 5:9–10; 2 Corinthians 5:18–19; Ephesians 2:13–17; Colossians 1:21, 23; Hebrews 2:17)

THE "QUIET" DISCIPLES

SCRIPTURES REFERENCED:
MATTHEW 10:1–4; MARK 3:16–19; LUKE 6:12–16; LUKE 5:8–10; JOHN 14:22; JOHN
1:43–49; JOHN 6:1–9; JOHN 14:6–9; JOHN 20:24–29; MARK 3:17; MARK 10:35–45;
ACTS 12:1–2; ACTS 17:1–6

That Jesus had twelve disciples is pretty well-known. That Peter and John were among them and that Judas Iscariot is the one who betrayed Jesus are also common knowledge. To go much beyond that, though, the details get a little murkier.

NINE MEN OUT

You can't tell the players without a scorecard, they say, so here's the remainder of the disciples' dozen:

- Andrew, brother of Peter;
- James, son of Zebedee, brother of John, and (with John) business partner of Peter;
- Philip, not the deacon from the book of Acts;
- Bartholomew, possibly also known as Nathanael;
- Thomas, of "Doubting Thomas" fame;
- Matthew, tax collector turned apostle and biblical writer;
- James, son of Alphaeus;
- Thaddeus, probably also known as Judas, a son of James; and
- Simon, nicknamed "The Zealot."

Oddly, though these men lived with, worked beside, and studied under Jesus for an extended time, we "hear" very little from them in the Bible.

With Jesus in their group, the disciples didn't have much chance of individual attention. But each of them would have been the focus of His attention. This painting dates to 1511.

FAMOUS LAST (OR ONLY) WORDS

While the first Gospel carries Matthew's name, nothing that he *said* is recorded anywhere in scripture. Simon the Zealot and James, son of Alphaeus, are also silent, though the latter seems to gain mention later in the New Testament as a church leader.

Thaddeus, likely identified as Judas (not Iscariot) in John's Gospel, utters a single Bible quotation: "But, Lord, why do you intend to show yourself to us and not to the world?"

Bartholomew, apparently called Nathanael by John, is best remembered for a snide remark about Jesus' hometown. The very day he received his call from Jesus, Philip was already spreading the good news. Finding Nathanael, Philip blurted, "We have found the one Moses wrote about in the Law, and about whom the prophets also wrote—Jesus of Nazareth, the son of Joseph." Bartholomew/Nathanael's response? "Nazareth! Can anything good come from there?" Philip just encouraged Nathanael to "come and see"—and when Jesus surprised Nathanael with His divine knowledge, the skeptic quickly changed his tune. "Rabbi, you are the Son of God," Nathanael marveled, "you are the king of Israel." That sentence constitutes Nathanael's last words in the Bible.

Philip will be heard from another time or two, first when he wondered how on earth Jesus planned to feed five thousand hungry men (plus an unnumbered group of women and children) who were listening to His preaching. "It would take more than half a year's wages to buy enough bread for each one to have a bite!" Philip told Jesus, who already had other plans (see "There *Is* Such a Thing as a Free Lunch" on page 72). At this point, Andrew delivers one of his handful of biblical lines: "Here is a boy with five small barley loaves and two small fish, but how far will they go among so many?"

Philip's final quotation occurs during Jesus' final hours with the disciples, before the Lord's arrest and crucifixion. After Jesus pronounced Himself "the way and the truth and the life," adding that "no one comes to the Father except through me," Philip said, "Lord, show us the Father and that will be enough for us." Jesus' response: "Don't you know me, Philip, even after I have been among you such a long time? Anyone who has seen me has seen the Father."

For Thomas, seeing wasn't enough—he wanted to touch Jesus before he'd believe the story of the Lord's resurrection. The man also known as "Didymus" (which means *twin*) uttered a few lines in the book of John, but none more famous than his "Unless I see the nail marks in his hands and put my finger where the nails were, and put my hand into his side, I will not believe." When Jesus appeared and invited Thomas to do just what he'd suggested, Thomas breathed out his "famous last words": "My Lord and my God!"

JESUS' POST-RESURRECTION APPEARANCES

- To Mary Magdalene outside the empty tomb (Mark 16:9–11)
- To the other women (Matthew 28:9–10)
- To two disciples on the road to Emmaus (Luke 24:13–32)
- To the eleven remaining apostles (Luke 24:36)
- To Peter (Luke 24:34; 1 Corinthians 15:5)
- To the apostles except for Thomas (John 20:19–25)
- To the eleven apostles (John 20:26–31)
- At seven apostles at the Sea of Galilee (John 21:1–23)
- To five hundred brothers (1 Corinthians 15:6)
- To the eleven apostles in Galilee (Matthew 28:16–20)
- To James (1 Corinthians 15:7)
- At the time of His ascension (Luke 24:36–50)
- To Paul at his conversion (Acts 9:1–19; 1 Corinthians 15:8)

Ancient Emmaus today. Two disciples were walking to this area when the resurrected Jesus joined them—but they didn't realize who He was until they stopped in the town for dinner.

JAMES, THE TRAILBLAZER

James was part of Jesus' inner circle of three, joining his brother John and business partner Peter in some of the Lord's most memorable experiences, like the Transfiguration. But in spite of his special status, James is quoted only a single time in the Bible, along with his brother John. The two men Jesus had called the "sons of thunder" pulled the Lord aside privately to say, "Teacher, we want you to do for us whatever we ask." What they asked

A Russian artist of the nineteenth-century painted this scene of Andrew—Peter's quiet brother—preaching in the Ukraine. Tradition says he planted a cross on the banks of the Dnieper River near modern-day Kiev. His death, according to legend, was on an X-shaped cross in the Peloponnese.

was rather brash: "Let one of us sit at your right and the other at your left in your glory."

When Jesus suggested that James and John didn't know what they were asking and questioned whether they could suffer the way He would suffer shortly, James spoke his final line in scripture: "We can." Jesus declined their request but did promise them trials: "You will drink the cup I drink and be baptized with the baptism I am baptized with."

Though he was a man of few recorded words, James's last biblical act spoke volumes: At the hands of the evil king Herod Agrippa I, James became the first of Jesus' twelve disciples to be martyred—and the only one specifically mentioned in scripture.

According to ancient tradition, though, he wouldn't be the last.

"Doubting Thomas," some say, spread the Gospel eastward before being killed by a dart in India. The former taxman Matthew suffered a similar fate in Africa, being run through with a spear. Andrew and Simon the Zealot were among those believed to be crucified, and Philip suffered the double jeopardy of stoning and crucifixion.

WALK THE TALK

Though we often lack information on what the disciples said, we certainly know what they *did*—in the King James Version language of a Thessalonian mob, stirring up trouble for the missionaries Paul and Silas, they "turned the world upside down."

Actions generally do speak louder than words.

PROPHET MARRIES A PROSTITUTE!

SCRIPTURES REFERENCED:
1 TIMOTHY 3:8–11; HOSEA 1–3; 2 KINGS 9:30–37; MICAH 7:18

The wives of church leaders, according to the apostle Paul, are to be "women. . .worthy of respect." So why on earth did a prophet named Hosea marry a prostitute?

WHO TOLD HIM TO?

Actually, this hook-up wasn't Hosea's idea. It was God's.

"Go, marry a promiscuous woman and have children with her," the Lord said. Hosea, God's spokesman to the northern Jewish kingdom of Israel, was being prepped for a theatrical performance worthy of a seventh-century BC Oscar.

Hosea would play the part of a faithful husband (a role based on God Himself) while his wife, Gomer (there's no "Pyle" at the end), would act the part of adulterous Israel. Sadly, Gomer's adultery was anything but pretend.

BABY NAMES

Like Israel wandering away from God, Gomer would stray from Hosea—but not before she bore him three oddly named kids. The inspiration for those names came, once again, from God Himself.

- *Baby #1:* Hosea called him *Jezreel*. It was a grisly name, relating to a place where some truly icky things had happened. For one thing, Jezebel was stomped to death by horses and eaten by dogs there (see "What a Way to Go" on page 100). For another, seventy descendants of Jezebel and her wicked husband, King Ahab, got their heads together there. What's gross about that, you ask? Well, it was literally just their *heads*—arriving in baskets at the command of a future Israelite king, Jehu.
- *Baby #2:* Hosea called her *Lo-Ruhamah*. It's actually kind of pretty the way it rolls off your tongue. But it means "not loved."
- *Baby #3:* Hosea called him *Lo-Ammi*, and (no surprise here) this name also had a dreary meaning, translating as "not my people."

Each of Hosea's kids was a walking billboard of God's judgment: "Call him Jezreel, because I will soon punish the house of Jehu for the massacre at Jezreel, and I will put an end to the kingdom of Israel. . . . Call her Lo-Ruhamah. . .for I will no longer show love to Israel. . . . Call him Lo-Ammi. . .for you are not my people, and I am not your God."

DON'T FORGET MOM

Motherhood apparently didn't suit Gomer, because before long she ran away from home. Hosea apparently found her in a slave market, since he had to pay both silver and grain to bring her back.

And, yet again, God was behind Hosea's next action: "Go, show your love to your wife again, though she is loved by another and is an adulteress," God said. "Love her as the LORD loves the Israelites, though they turn to other gods and love the sacred raisin cakes."

Hosea did, but he also gave Gomer a stern warning: "You are to live with me many days; you must not be a prostitute or be intimate with any man, and I will behave the same way toward you."

A HAPPY ENDING?

Clearly, this was not the perfect Cleaver family of 1950s television—but, ultimately, there would be a happy ending. We've already dropped hints as to what it is.

Though God was royally ticked with the people of Israel—and used Hosea's family to act out their shortcomings—He still loved His people: "Yet the Israelites will be like the sand on the seashore, which cannot be measured or counted. In the place where it was said to them, 'You are not my people,' they will be called 'children of the living God.'"

No wonder another prophet, Micah, wrote of the Lord, "Who is a God like you, who pardons sin and forgives the transgression of the remnant of his inheritance? You do not stay angry forever, but delight to show mercy."

WHAT WE KNOW ABOUT HOSEA

- Hosea was the son of a man named Beeri.
- Hosea's name means "May the Lord save" or "Deliverance."
- Hosea was probably from the nation of Israel, maybe Samaria. He regarded Israel his homeland.
- Hosea was married to a prostitute named Gomer and had three children: sons Jezreel and Lo-Ammi and daughter Lo-Ruhamah.
- Hosea ministered about 2750 years ago, during the reigns of the last two kings of Israel, shortly before Israel was destroyed by the Assyrian Empire (c. 722 BC). He prophesied during the concluding years of King Jeroboam II.
- His book is the first of the twelve "Minor Prophets" and the longest.
- Hosea loved the nation of Israel but saw her as corrupt, evil, and wayward. His prophecies referred to the judgments that would come upon Israel as a result of the people's unfaithfulness to God, but they also include God's promise to restore the nation.
- Hosea is well-known for his terrible home life. His wife's unfaithfulness was a picture of the unfaithfulness of the nation of Israel. Just as Gomer had left home for a life of prostitution, Israel had turned away from God to pursue false gods. Despite his wife's unfaithfulness, Hosea continued to love her, pursue her, and bring her home—just as God continue to love Israel.

Hosea, as imagined by an Italian artist of the fourteenth century.

LOOK WHO'S TALKING

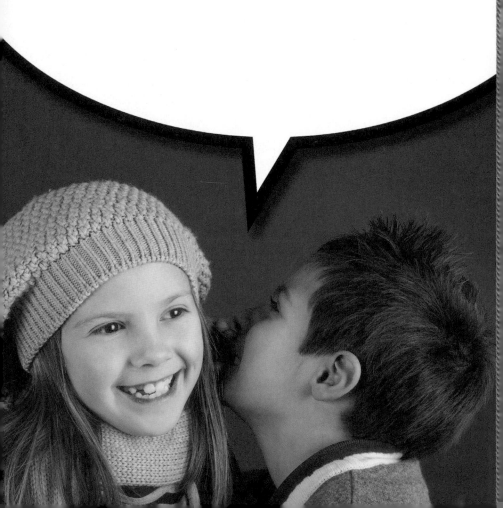

Smile. . .
God loves you.

SCRIPTURES REFERENCED:
GENESIS 3; NUMBERS 22–23; EXODUS 3; 1 CORINTHIANS 1:21; 2 CORINTHIANS 11:14; ISAIAH 8:19–20

Human beings occupy the pinnacle of life on earth. Disregarding for the moment most of what appears on television these days, humans are clearly the highest form of life, greater than any other organism in feats of intellect, creativity, and communication.

Regarding the latter, humans are unique in their ability to string together particular sounds in patterns recognizable to both sender and receiver. That's called *speech*—and it's an exclusively human talent.

WELL, MAYBE NOT. . .

Okay, so there's an exception to most every rule. In the Bible, you'll find a couple of cases of *animals* talking—clearly interacting with the "more advanced" human beings around them. And for you skeptics out there, these weren't the hokey special effects of the old *Mr. Ed* television show.

Exhibit #1: A serpent, slithering up to Eve in the Garden of Eden, spoke a few words that spelled the downfall of the entire human race: "Did God really say, 'You must not eat from any tree in the garden'? . . . You will not certainly die. . . . For God knows that when you eat from it your eyes will be opened, and you will be like God, knowing good and evil."

The serpent that deceived Eve may not have looked like the snakes we know today—because God's punishment included the curse "you will crawl on your belly" (Genesis 3:14).

How would a serpent speak? According to the Bible's book of Genesis, the creature was "more crafty than any of the wild animals the LORD God had made." And, it seems clear, it was being used—possessed even, by the fallen angel Satan—to bring about humankind's doom.

For shooting off its mouth, the serpent paid a heavy price: God cursed the creature "above all livestock and all wild animals," ordering the serpent to crawl on its belly and eat dust as long as it lived.

BIBLICAL NAMES OF THE DEVIL

- Abaddon (Revelation 9:11)
- Accuser (Revelation 12:10)
- Adversary (1 Peter 5:8 KJV)
- Ancient serpent (Revelation 12:9)
- Angel of light (2 Corinthians 11:14)
- Angel of the Abyss (Revelation 9:11)
- Apollyon (Revelation 9:11)
- Beelzebul (Matthew 12:24)
- Belial (2 Corinthians 6:15)
- Deceiver (Revelation 12:9 KJV)
- Devil (1 John 3:8)
- Dragon (Revelation 12:9)
- Enemy (Matthew 13:39)
- Evil one (Ephesians 6:16; John 17:15)
- Father of lies (John 8:44)
- God of this age (2 Corinthians 4:4)
- King of the bottomless pit (Revelation 9:11 KJV)
- Liar (John 8:44)
- Lucifer (Isaiah 14:12–14 KJV)
- Man of lawlessness (2 Thessalonians 2:3–4)
- Murderer (John 8:44)
- Prince of demons (Luke 11:15)
- Prince of this world (John 12:31–32)
- Roaring lion (1 Peter 5:8)
- Ruler of the kingdom of the air (Ephesians 2:1–2)
- Satan (Mark 1:13)
- Tempter (Matthew 4:3)
- Thief (John 10:10)

The classic allegory of John Bunyan, *The Pilgrim's Progress*, uses the name Apollyon for its Satan character.

Exhibit #2: A donkey debated its owner, a man named Balaam, who didn't seem to think it odd to be talking with an animal. Balaam, a prophet of God, had angered the Lord—maybe by wanting a bribe offered him by the king of Moab, who urged Balaam to curse God's people, the Israelites.

On his way to meet the Moabite king, with his donkey acting strangely, Balaam lost his cool. On a narrow pathway, the animal pressed close to the wall, crushing Balaam's foot, and then lay down in the path and refused to move. When Balaam resorted to beating the poor creature with a stick, God caused the donkey to speak: "What have I done to you to make you beat me these three times?"

His donkey is talking and there's an angel with a sword who came within a whisker of killing him. Is it any wonder Balaam looks confused?

Balaam was so mad he was oblivious to the strange situation taking place—and he promptly answered the donkey. "You have made a fool of me!" he shouted. "If only I had a sword in my hand, I would kill you right now."

Showing far more reason than its human owner, the donkey then asked Balaam, "Am I not your own donkey, which you have always ridden, to this day? Have I been in the habit of doing this to you?"

The prophet had to admit that his donkey had not acted that way before—at which point, he realized *why* the animal had done what it had done. "Then the LORD opened Balaam's eyes, and he saw the angel of the LORD standing in the road with his sword drawn."

SPEAKING WITHOUT A MOUTH

Though it must have been strange to see animals speak, at least they had mouths with which to do so. Moses once heard a voice coming from a bush.

It wasn't just any bush, and it wasn't just any voice, either. The bush was burning, but it never burned up. The voice was that of God Himself.

"Moses, Moses!" the bush said.

Moses answered, "Here I am."

"Do not come any closer," the bush commanded. "Take off your sandals, for the place where you are standing is holy ground."

At that point, the voice in the bush identified itself: "I am the God of your father, the God of Abraham, the God of Isaac and the God of Jacob."

ESAIAS

Michelangelo's Sistine Chapel portrait of the prophet Isaiah, whose tongue was purified by a heavenly coal applied by an angel (Isaiah 6:6). For around forty years, Isaiah spoke God's words to God's people.

LISTEN UP

God can use anything He wants to get his message across—whether it's a bush, a donkey, or even the "foolishness of what was preached," to use the apostle Paul's phrase. On the other hand, Satan can speak through various objects, too, so be careful. That's part of the devil's propensity to masquerade as "an angel of light."

So how can you know which voice to believe?

The answer is straightforward: You just need to compare what you hear with the Word of God, the Bible. Here's how the prophet Isaiah put it:

When someone tells you to consult mediums and spiritists, who whisper and mutter, should not a people inquire of their God? Why consult the dead on behalf of the living? Consult God's instruction and the testimony of warning. If anyone does not speak according to this word, they have no light of dawn.

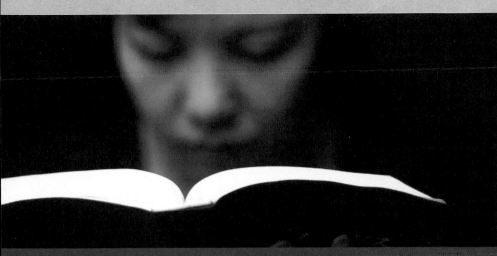

HOW GOD SPEAKS TO US TODAY

Many folks, including Bible-believing Christians, wonder if God still speaks to people today—and if so, how? The answer to the first question is an emphatic *yes*! God wants His people to hear from Him—to seek to know His thoughts and His ways.

But how does God speak to us? It's possible (but uncommon) that people will hear the audible voice of God today. God clearly prefers to "speak" through His written Word. Second Timothy 3:16–17 tells us, "All Scripture is God-breathed and is useful for teaching, rebuking, correcting and training in righteousness, so that the servant of God may be thoroughly equipped for every good work." This simply means that the Bible contains everything you need to live the Christian life, simply because it contains the words and thoughts of God Himself.

God also speaks to us today through our impressions and thoughts and through certain events. The Bible teaches that God helps us to know right from wrong through our consciences (see 1 Timothy 1:5 and 1 Peter 3:16).

God allows events to occur in our lives to direct us, change us, and help us to grow spiritually (see James 1:2–5 and Hebrews 12:5–11).

But how can we know if what we think is the voice of God speaking to us really is His voice? And how can we know if the impressions, thoughts, and events we experience really are from God? It's simple. If the voice we hear or the thoughts or impressions we experience line up with what the Bible says, then they can be trusted. If they don't, they can't.

So trust, above all things, the Word of God!

BIBLICAL TWINS—AND TRIPLETS?

SCRIPTURES REFERENCED:
GENESIS 25:19–32; GENESIS 38; GENESIS 5:32

The Bible often reads like the "New Arrivals" section of a small-town newspaper. Births are detailed—from Isaac to Moses to Jesus, along with scores of others—many times with a brief description of the happy parents.

DOUBLY BLESSED

On certain occasions, one baby just wasn't enough: The Bible records two instances of the birth of twins. You may already be thinking of one pair—Jacob and Esau—but if this author were a betting man (which he isn't), he might lay a wager you couldn't identify the other.

Famous guys first: Esau and Jacob, to note their proper birth order, were the sons and grandsons of Israel's great patriarchs Isaac and Abraham. A case of sibling rivalry started early—the babies "jostled each other" inside

The ultrasound came thousands of years after Perez and Zerah—but if Tamar were expecting today, her biblical twins would look something like this.

their mother Rebekah—and would ultimately lead to the younger brother stealing his older bro's birthright. Though there would be some pretty tense moments, their rivalry wouldn't reach the dizzying heights of certain other biblical siblings (see "Sibling Rivalry to the Extreme" on page 114).

The Bible's other twins? Perez and Zerah, the dynamic duo born to a woman named Tamar and her father-in-law, Judah, who mistook her for a prostitute (see "Bad Apples on Jesus' Family Tree" on page 86). Zerah thought he was the older brother but then changed his mind: He stuck his hand out first, long enough for a midwife to tie a scarlet thread around his wrist, before pulling himself fully back into the womb. Perez, whose name means "breaking out," then emerged to lay claim to the big sib status.

THREE'S COMPANY

You won't find the word *triplet* in most reputable Bible translations, though you might—by reading between the lines—find a case of three babies born at once. As with the two sets of twins, the story happens in the bedrock book of Genesis.

Undoubtedly, you know the father: a guy named Noah. And you've likely heard of his sons: Shem, Ham, and Japheth, quite possibly the world's first recorded set of triplets.

In a genealogical listing of humanity's earliest generations, the King James Version of Genesis notes, "And Noah was five hundred years old; and Noah begat Shem, Ham, and Japheth." There are only two ways that three boys could be born in one year: Either they all came together as triplets, or they split up two and one, with the Bible's third set of twins and a solitary brother appearing in rapid succession.

In the New International Version of the Bible, the verse in question says the famous ark builder became the father of the three boys "*after* Noah was 500 years old" (emphasis added). If that's a truer translation of the original language, the triplet idea loses some of its vigor.

No one can say for sure, but isn't it fun to speculate?

MURDEROUS INTENT

SCRIPTURES REFERENCED:
EXODUS 2:11–4:31; 1 SAMUEL 13:13–14; 2 SAMUEL 11–12; MATTHEW 5:21–24; LUKE 9:51–56; EXODUS 33:11; PSALM 51; ACTS 12:1–4

Conduct a poll on "the worst sin," and chances are most people will answer "murder." So do you find it a little bit shocking that some of the Bible's greatest leaders had murder in their hearts—even blood on their hands?

THE (UN)USUAL SUSPECTS

Here's a police lineup for you: Moses, David, and James and John. We don't have their mug shots, but we do have a clear record of their homicidal tendencies.

Moses, chosen by God to lead the Israelites out of their slavery in Egypt, resisted that call—perhaps because he was a wanted man. Years before, as an Israelite adopted into the pharaoh's family, Moses had killed a fellow Egyptian with his own hands, then "hid him in the sand." When Moses realized he'd been found out, he ran away to avoid Egyptian justice, returning to the African nation only after God assured him, "All those who wanted to kill you are dead."

David was Israel's greatest king, once described as "a man after [God's] own heart" by the prophet Samuel. But there was nothing Godlike in David's adulterous pursuit of a married woman, nor in his scheme to knock off her husband. After satisfying his desires with the beautiful Bathsheba, David tried to make her resulting pregnancy look like the work of her husband, Uriah. But Uriah wouldn't play along—David called him back from the army to spend time with his wife, but the honorable soldier said he couldn't do that while his comrades were facing the enemy in the field. Thus thwarted, David got desperate—hatching a plan to eliminate Uriah and take his wife for keeps. "Put Uriah out in front where the fighting is fiercest," David wrote to his military commander, Joab. "Then withdraw from him so he will be struck down and die."

James and John didn't actually kill anyone, though they once wanted to wipe out an entire Samaritan village. And in the view of Jesus, the teacher they followed, that kind of anger was essentially murder. The disciple brothers were offended when these particular Samaritans refused to welcome Jesus, who was traveling through on His way to Jerusalem. "Lord," they asked, "do you want us to call fire down from heaven to destroy them?" Even an atheist could tell you that's not what Jesus was about, so He scolded the two disciples and moved on.

WHO WERE JAMES AND JOHN?

- The two were sons of Zebedee, a prominent Galilean fisherman, and Salome.
- Their hometown was Capernaum.
- Some scholars speculate that James and John may have been cousins of Jesus.
- James and John became Jesus' disciples when the Master called the brothers to leave their fishing boat and follow Him.
- They were among the twelve Jesus called to be His apostles.
- In his Gospel, John frequently refers to himself as "the disciple whom Jesus loved," indicating an especially close relationship with the Lord.
- Jairus's daughter and the Transfiguration of Jesus.
- When a Samaritan village rejected Jesus, James and John wanted Him to call down fire from heaven to destroy the place. This earned a nickname from Jesus: *Boanerges*, or "sons of thunder."
- James and John's mother overstepped her bounds when she asked Jesus to grant her sons a special place in His kingdom.
- James was killed by the sword by Herod, making him the first martyred apostle (Acts 12:2).
- John wrote a Gospel, three letters that bear his name, and

AH, REDEMPTION

Thankfully, no one—not even a murderer—is beyond the reach of God's grace.

Putting his youthful violence behind him, Moses ultimately accepted God's call to lead the Israelites. (Though, truth be told, he probably wanted to kill *them* on several occasions.) The former Egyptian prince became one of the greatest leaders in Israel's history, one that God "would speak to. . .face to face, as one speaks to a friend."

It took a tear-jerking story from the prophet Nathan to make David repent of his sin against Uriah. When the king heard a parable of a rich man who made a meal of his poor neighbor's only lamb—a lamb, in fact, that was more like a daughter than a bit of livestock—David was cut to the bone by Nathan's accusation, "You are the man!" In time, David would pour out his soul in one of the Bible's greatest psalms, the fifty-first:

> *Have mercy on me, O God,*
> *according to your unfailing love;*
> *according to your great compassion*
> *blot out my transgressions. . . .*
>
> *For I know my transgressions,*
> *and my sin is always before me.*
> *Against you, you only, have I sinned*
> *and done what is evil in your sight. . . .*
>
> *Create in me a pure heart, O God,*
> *and renew a steadfast spirit within me.*

As professional fishermen in a family business that included their father, Zebedee, James and John must have had their future clearly planned—until Jesus made them fishers of men.

And then there were James and John, who finally "got it," understanding that Jesus' agenda was not vengeance but mercy. In writing the three letters we now know as 1, 2, and 3 John, the one-time wannabe executioner spoke more than forty times of *love*. His brother, meanwhile, would become the first of Jesus' twelve disciples to be put to death for the cause (see "The 'Quiet' Disciples" on page 218).

A LITTLE PERSPECTIVE

As sins go, murder is definitely one of the biggies, warranting a mention in God's ultimate list of no-nos, the Ten Commandments. But those regulations also prohibit such "little" sins as stealing, lying, even wanting things that belong to other people.

The fact is that *every* sin offends God—and even if you've never killed anyone, you've certainly broken any number of the remaining nine commandments. Does that sound hopeless? It is—until Jesus enters the picture. But through Him, anyone and everyone has an opportunity for redemption.

And aren't you glad for that?

PAUL'S MESSAGE OF HOPE

It's the most wonderful of all Bible curiosities, God's grace and forgiveness for sinners. The apostle Paul had a lot to say about God's grace as well as the sin it covers. Writing to the church at Corinth, he laid out a list of people who would not inherit God's kingdom but would be lost for all eternity. This list is found in 1 Corinthians 6:9–11, and it looks like this:

- the sexually immoral
- idolaters
- adulterers
- men who have sex with men
- thieves
- the greedy
- drunkards
- slanderers
- swindlers

When we read that passage, it might be tempting to think, *I'm none of those things, so I must be doing all right!* But Paul didn't intend to provide a comprehensive list of sinners who would spend eternity in "the other place"—notice that the word *murderers* is nowhere to be found in this passage—he was simply making the point that the wicked would never make it to heaven. Besides, we humans can be very creative when it comes to finding things to do that offend God.

The apostle Paul, as envisioned by the sixteenth-century painter El Greco.

The good news in this passage is found in verse 11: "And that is what some of you *were*. But you were washed, you were sanctified, you were justified in the name of the Lord Jesus Christ and by the Spirit of our God" (italics added).

God's grace really is amazing, isn't it?

SURF GALILEE

SCRIPTURES REFERENCED:
MATTHEW 14:22–36; MARK 6:45–56; JOHN 6:16–24

The sport of surfing was unknown in Jesus' time. But His famous stroll on the Sea of Galilee brings that California pastime to mind.

IT WAS A DARK AND STORMY NIGHT

Most everyone knows that Jesus "walked on water"—it's a phrase used to describe people who do things perfectly (or who like to *think* they do) and an image occasionally spoofed in advertisements and movies.

Here's exactly what happened: Right after feeding the five thousand (see "There *Is* Such a Thing as a Free Lunch" on page 72), Jesus shipped off His disciples—literally. "Jesus made his disciples get into the boat and go on ahead of him to Bethsaida, while he dismissed the crowd," reported the Bible writer Mark. While the disciples took a ride, Jesus took a leave—going into the hills to pray.

For the Twelve, it was tough going. A stiff wind opposed their rowing, throwing up waves that rocked the boat over the course of three grueling miles. As darkness fell and the wind continued to howl, the disciples fought with their oars—when suddenly Jesus made one of the oddest stage

The story is told so often that its impact has often been lost on its hearers. But just try walking on the sea yourself!

entrances in the theater of history: "They saw Jesus approaching the boat, walking on the water."

We know it was nighttime, and we can guess that the windy storm obscured the moon and stars—so the disciples' view of Jesus was probably by the light of a lamp or two attached to their boat. The mariners' reaction was understandable considering the spooky circumstances: "They thought he was a ghost. . .and were terrified."

CATCHIN' A WAVE

Walking on water (unfrozen water, of course) is a truly amazing thing. But before we delve further into the miracle, consider for a moment the path Jesus took to get to His disciples. This was no placid lake with a smooth, easy surface. It was a roiling, crashing sea in the midst of a windstorm.

Jesus must have walked up, up, and up the fronts of waves like He was on a first-century Stairmaster—then perhaps surfed down the other side as the billows crested. If that sounds like a killer workout, remember that Jesus was accustomed to hiking most everywhere He went, often in very hilly country.

Close enough now to talk with His disciples, Jesus called out, "Take courage! It is I. Don't be afraid." And at that point, the miracle was doubled.

GOOD OLD PETER

That most impetuous of disciples, Simon Peter, seized the moment, telling the ghost who claimed to be Jesus, "Lord, if it's you. . .tell me to come to you on the water." The Lord's response was simple: "Come."

For a glorious moment, Peter was the only human being not named "Jesus" ever to walk on water. When a gusty wind shook his confidence, though, Peter took his eyes off the Lord—and quickly did what all other feet-first people do in water. Sink.

A three-word prayer erupted from Peter's lips: "Lord, save me!" Saving, of course, is Jesus' main business, and the Lord quickly caught Peter by the hand, pulling him back to the surface. With a small scolding ("You of little faith. . . why did you doubt?"), Jesus helped Peter into the boat—which immediately, miraculously, appeared on the other side of the lake in a perfect calm.

AND NOW, FOR THE APPLICATION. . .

Sometimes your life is the Sea of Galilee—very dark, stormy, and scary. Jesus comes to you in a surprising way, helping you do things you never thought possible and saving you when you think you're drowning. And then He brings calm.

Just think of that the next time you wax your surfboard.

JESUS WAS HERE

- Bethany (Matthew 26:6)
- Bethlehem (Matthew 2:1)
- Bethphage (Matthew 21:1)
- Calvary (Luke 23:33 KJV)
- Cana (John 2:11)
- Capernaum (Matthew 4:13)
- Damascus area (Acts 9:1–5)
- Egypt (Matthew 2:14)
- Gabbatha (John 19:13)
- Gethsemane (Matthew 26:36)
- Golgotha (Mark 15:22)
- Heaven (Acts 7:56)
- Jacob's well (John 4:6)
- Jerusalem (Mark 11:11)
- Mount of Olives (John 8:1)
- Nain (Luke 7:11)
- Nazareth (Matthew 2:23)
- Peter's house (Matthew 8:14)
- Praetorium (Mark 15:16)
- Samaria (Luke 17:11)
- Sea of Galilee (Matthew 4:18)
- Sychar (John 4:5)
- Synagogue (Luke 4:16)
- Temple (Matthew 21:12)
- Upper room (Mark 14:15)

UFO FILES

SCRIPTURES REFERENCED:
EZEKIEL 1, 37

Long before Roswell, New Mexico, and Area 51, there were the close encounters of the prophet Ezekiel. If you like stories of mysterious extraterrestrials, check this out.

IT'S KIND OF HARD TO EXPLAIN

"Bizarre" well describes what the thirty-year-old Jewish exile saw in Babylonia. About six hundred years before Christ, Ezekiel got a call to speak God's Word to the rebellious people of Israel, who had been carried off by an enemy army to the area of modern-day Iraq. How God chose to get Ezekiel's attention is a classic oddity of the Bible.

A windstorm was brewing in the north, and Ezekiel reported a huge cloud flashing lightning. Brilliant light shone around the cloud, and a fire, glowing like molten metal, illuminated four extraterrestrials—which Ezekiel called "living creatures." But these weren't your traditional "little green men" he saw.

The Ishtar Gate of ancient Babylon, re-constructed inside a German museum, was built around the time Ezekiel prophesied to God's exiled people.

A PROPHET AHEAD OF HIS TIME

The prophet Ezekiel ministered to the people of Israel from around 593–571 BC. During that time, the people were being held captive in Babylon in what is called the "Babylonian Captivity."

The book of Ezekiel is seen as a companion to the book of Revelation. Several of Ezekiel's prophecies are mirrored in Revelation, including:

- the "living creatures" (Ezekiel 1, Revelation 4)
- eating the scroll (Ezekiel 3, Revelation 10)
- Gog and Magog (Ezekiel 38, Revelation 20)
- the river of living water (Ezekiel 47, Revelation 22)
- the New Jerusalem (Ezekiel 40–48, Revelation 22).

Each of the living creatures resembled a man, but with four faces—one human, one like a lion, one like an ox, and the last like an eagle. Each had feet that looked like polished brass, in the shape of calves' hooves. And each had multiple wings, some with which they flew and others with which they covered themselves. Underneath the wings were human hands. If that's not odd enough, each of the living creatures glowed like fire, zipping around with the speed and appearance of lightning.

These four-faced, multiwinged ETs were also accompanied by some kind of strange vessel, perhaps a type of BC UFO. "As I looked at the living creatures," Ezekiel said, "I saw a wheel on the ground beside each creature with its four faces." Each disk (a kind of flying saucer?) stood out in 3–D, as one wheel intersected another. Rimming the circumference of each wheel were—get this—*eyes*.

The sparkling, greenish-yellow wheels moved as the living creatures moved, side to side, back and forth, up and down. The mysterious pairs were connected by some kind of mind control, Ezekiel said, "because the spirit of the living creatures was in the wheels."

VISIONS R US

Truth be told, UFOs and extraterrestrials weren't the most unusual thing Ezekiel saw in his days as a prophet. There was also the time God showed our friend Zeke a valley full of old, dry human bones.

"Can these bones live?" God asked Ezekiel, who responded very wisely, "Sovereign LORD, you alone know."

God told Ezekiel to prophesy to the bones, surely one of the quietest audiences he'd ever appeared before. "Dry bones, hear the word of the LORD! This is what the Sovereign LORD says to these bones: I will make breath enter you and you will come to life. I will attach tendons to you and make flesh come upon you and cover you with skin; I will put breath in you, and you will come to life. Then you will know that I am the LORD."

That said, the bones were no longer quiet. With a rattling noise, they began to move and come together, the hip bone connected to the leg bone, the leg bone connected to the knee bone, and so on and so on until an army of skeletons lay before Ezekiel. Then, as God had said, tendons began to grow on the bones, followed by flesh and skin until entire human bodies appeared. This reverse decomposition stopped at the point of actual resurrection, though: "There was no breath in them," Ezekiel wrote.

The breath would come soon enough, upon Ezekiel's next prophecy. "This is what the Sovereign LORD says: Come, breath, from the four winds, and breathe into these slain, that they may live." And that's exactly what happened, as suddenly a vast army of living people came to life and rose to their feet.

Human bones stored under a Czech church. Ezekiel had a vision of an entire valley full of skeletons.

WHAT DOES IT ALL MEAN?

Everything Ezekiel saw and shared with the Israelites was designed to point them back to God—the God they'd been disobeying, disrespecting, and disappointing for generations. But God still wanted to show His people mercy.

Ezekiel's close encounter of the third kind was designed to reveal God to him—because above the living creatures was "something like a vault, sparkling like crystal, and awesome." Above the expanse he saw "what looked like a throne of lapis lazuli, and high above on the throne was a figure like that of a man." Most likely Jesus Christ Himself, the figure appeared from "his waist up. . .like glowing metal, as if full of fire, and. . .from there down he looked like fire; and brilliant light surrounded him. Like the appearance of a rainbow in the clouds on a rainy day, so was the radiance around him."

When the prophet saw "dem bones, dem bones, dem dry bones," God was making a promise to His chosen people. "Son of man," God told Ezekiel, "these bones are the people of Israel. They say, 'Our bones are dried up and our hope is gone; we are cut off.' Therefore prophesy and say to them, 'This is what the Sovereign LORD says: My people, I am going to open your graves and bring you up from them; I will bring you back to the land of Israel.'"

IT'S JUST SO STRANGE

Well, sure it is. But no stranger than God's continual mercy for His people. Whether it makes sense to us is less important than the fact that God is going out of His way to show His love.

Hard to understand? You bet. But definitely something to believe in.

A GLANCE AT THE MAN NAMED EZEKIEL

- Ezekiel was the son of a priest named Buzi (Ezekiel 1:3). The name Ezekiel literally means "God strengthens."
- Ezekiel was among the people of Israel taken to Babylon. When he lived in Israel, he was a priest in Jerusalem.
- Ezekiel was near the Kebar River in Mesopotamia when he saw a prophetic vision of God and His cherubim (Ezekiel 1:1).
- God called Ezekiel to prophesy through a vision. God warned Ezekiel that he would be preaching to obstinate, stubborn people but that he was not to be afraid to speak to them.
- The number four (four living creatures, four wings, four faces, etc.) is important in the book of Ezekiel.
- When Ezekiel's wife died, he was not allowed to grieve or mourn.
- Like the prophet Jeremiah, Ezekiel recognized that God was using Babylon to bring judgment on His wayward people.
- After the fall of Jerusalem, the tone of Ezekiel's prophecies changes from those of doom to those of hope and encouragement.
- Ezekiel ministered from 593 to 571 BC. The Bible provides no information about him after the end of his ministry.

A sculpture of Ezekiel in France's Cathédrale Notre-Dame d'Amiens.

KING CONSULTS WITCH

SCRIPTURES REFERENCED:
EXODUS 22:18; 1 SAMUEL 10–19; 1 SAMUEL 28

Warty noses, lots of black clothing, and bubbling pots of newts' eyes, bats' teeth, and what-not make up the traditional Halloween picture of witches. They certainly wouldn't have been so flamboyant in Bible times, because God's rule on witches, spoken through Moses, was, "Do not allow a sorceress to live."

THERE'S ALWAYS SOMEONE

Skirting the rules is an activity as old as humanity itself (remember Adam and Eve eating that forbidden fruit?), and witchcraft never entirely went away. Even when Israel's first king, Saul, "expelled the mediums and spiritists from the land," at least one woman kept the dark arts going in a town called Endor, about fifty miles north of Jerusalem.

That's where Saul himself once traveled to find the woman—not to punish her for her illegal actions, but to ask for her help. The king wanted to consult the spirit of the dead prophet Samuel.

Saul, you may know, had been anointed king by Samuel and started his royal career in strong fashion by leading the Jewish army in a rout of the enemy Ammonites. But soon Saul was in Samuel's doghouse. The king tended to do things his own way, cutting corners on the rules both God and Samuel had laid down. There was the time the king made a burnt offering—a job reserved for priests alone. And there was another time when Saul was supposed to completely destroy the enemy Amalekites in battle but allowed their king and much of their livestock to live. When Samuel asked how the battle had gone, Saul fibbed, saying, "I have carried out the LORD's instructions." The prophet's reply would have been funny had it not been so sad: "What then is this bleating of sheep in my ears? What is this lowing of cattle that I hear?"

For those kinds of blunders, Saul lost his kingdom. God decided He would no longer support Saul, and He told Samuel to anoint a new king, David. Until David actually assumed power several years later, Saul found that God wasn't talking to him—not by dreams, prophets, or Urim, a mysterious object that God used to reveal His will. So, once again, the king bent the rules—and went searching for a witch.

WELCOME TO ENDOR

Royal robes were left behind for this trip. Saul disguised himself, though you have to wonder how effective any disguise would have been on him. One thing about Saul that impressed the Jewish people was his great height: "As he stood among the people he was a head taller than any of the others."

Apparently, the medium of Endor wasn't a psychic, because she didn't perceive who was standing at her door. She was wary, of course, when the stranger asked her to call up a spirit: "Surely you know what Saul has done," she said. "He has cut off the mediums and spiritists from the land."

Saul, still unrecognized, assured the woman that he was not laying a trap for her and asked to talk with Samuel. When Samuel's spirit actually materialized, looking like an old man in a robe, the witch screamed in fear—not of a dead man's spirit in her house, but of the very live king of Israel, whom she finally had figured out. "Why have you deceived me?" she wailed. "You are Saul!"

Saul's response: "Don't be afraid. What do you see?" Translation: "Focus, woman, focus."

Samuel's presence filled the room. Saul fell facedown in respect.

NOT WHAT HE WANTED TO HEAR

The old (and dead) prophet was not pleased.

"Why have you disturbed me by bringing me up?" Samuel demanded.

"I am in great distress," Saul answered, explaining his recent disconnect with the Lord. "God has departed from me. He no longer answers me, either by prophets or by dreams. So I have called on you to tell me what to do."

Samuel's answer was less "what to do" than "where to go." First, the prophet dropped a bombshell, telling Saul that God was taking the kingdom from Saul and his family and giving it instead to David. Then Samuel got to the *really* bad news: In an upcoming battle, "The LORD will deliver both Israel and you into the hands of the Philistines, and tomorrow you and your sons will be with me." (That means "dead," in case you're wondering.)

Since Samuel was a true prophet, his words were borne out exactly. Wounded in battle on Mount Gilboa, Saul actually fell on his own sword to avoid being tortured and abused by the Philistines. So ended Israel's first "dynasty."

THE MORAL OF THE STORY

Two wrongs (or three, or four, or twenty-seven) don't make a right. A string of bad decisions led Saul to the point of consulting with a witch—which turned out to be his final mistake.

THE HISTORY OF ISRAEL FROM THE EXODUS TO THE RETURN FROM BABYLONIAN CAPTIVITY

- c. 1500–1200 BC–Exodus and Promised Land Conquest (Late Bronze Age)
- c. 1492 BC–The Exodus from Egypt
- c. 1452 BC–Joshua appointed leader of the people of Israel
- c. 1451 BC–The crossing of the Jordan
- c. 1451–44 BC–Conquest of Canaan
- c. 1394–1095 BC–The period of the Judges
- c. 1095–1055 BC–King Saul, Israel's first monarch
- c. 1055–1015 BC–King David
- c. 1050 BC–Philistines settle in southern Palestine
- c. 1015–975 BC–King Solomon

- c. 1005 BC–Dedication of the temple
- c. 975–587 BC–The divided kingdom (Judah and Israel)
- c. 721 BC–Captivity of Israel
- c. 587 BC–Babylonian Captivity of Judah
- c. 535 BC–Return of the Jews to Jerusalem under Zerubbabel
- c. 515 BC–Second emple dedicated
- c. 458 BC–Ezra leads second wave of Jews back to Jerusalem
- c. 445 BC–Nehemiah returns to Jerusalem and begins rebuilding city walls

The faithful Jews who labored to rebuild Jerusalem's walls after the Babylonian captivity could never have imagined what the city would ultimately become.

PETER'S PRISON BREAK

SCRIPTURES REFERENCED:

ACTS 12:1–19; ISAIAH 61:1–2

*E*scape from Alcatraz it wasn't—but the apostle Peter's breakout from King Herod's prison boasts danger, intrigue, a dash of humor, and a miracle or two along the way.

VIOLATORS WILL BE PERSECUTED

Herod Agrippa I was a very bad man (see "What a Way to Go" on page 100) who lost no love on Christians. One year around Passover time, the king tried to impress Jewish leaders by seizing the apostle James (the brother of John) and having him executed. The Jews who hated this new "sect" called Christianity gave Herod's action two thumbs up—so the king had Peter arrested, too.

Guarded by sixteen soldiers—four squads of four men each—Peter undoubtedly sensed his own death rapidly approaching. But Herod's executioner didn't stand a chance against the earnest prayers of Peter's fellow believers.

On the eve of Peter's scheduled trial (even a rotten king had to keep up appearances, you know), the great apostle was calm enough to sleep. You'd think being chained to soldiers on either side would make for an uncomfortable snooze, but Peter was sleeping soundly. Additional soldiers,

This prisoner is under "light supervision" compared to the way Peter was guarded.

meanwhile, kept vigil in the prison doorway to keep Peter in and anybody else out.

Good luck barring the door to an angel.

THE RESCUE

Suddenly, Peter's darkened cell blazed with heavenly light, as an angel materialized to break Peter free. But first things first—the angel had to swat Peter on the side to rouse him from his slumber. "Quick, get up!" the angel said, and when Peter stood, the chains around his wrists simply fell off.

In a daze—he actually thought he was having a vision—Peter dressed and followed the angel past one guard, then another, then out of the prison. The two traipsed on toward one of the gates of Jerusalem, a large iron door that swung open all by itself, and continued into the city.

Peter finally snapped to when the angel disappeared. "Now I know without a doubt," he thought, "that the Lord has sent his angel and rescued me from Herod's clutches."

Because Jesus once told Peter, "I will give you the keys of the kingdom of heaven" (Matthew 16:19), many paintings and

A rendezvous with his fellow Christians was in order, so Peter headed for the home of one of the Bible's many Marys—this one, the mother of Gospel writer John Mark.

There were many people inside the house, but they weren't having a party. This was a prayer meeting—one that Peter was soon to disrupt.

THAT DASH OF HUMOR WE MENTIONED

Peter's pounding on an outer entryway caught the attention of a servant girl named Rhoda. When she realized a real, live answer to prayer was standing outside the house, she forgot her manners. Leaving Peter where he was, she ran to the assembled crowd to shout, "Peter is at the door!"

Showing very little faith in the power of their prayers, the people responded, "You're out of your mind." Don't you just love human nature?

Rhoda insisted that Peter was indeed out of jail and outside the home, at which point the pray-ers changed their tune—slightly. "It must be his angel," they intoned. And still they missed the entire point of their prayer meeting.

But Peter "got it" and kept pounding on the outer entryway. When someone finally opened the door, the believers actually believed—and Peter told them the whole story of his escape.

LET MY PEOPLE GO!

It shouldn't surprise us that God orchestrated a jail break, because the Lord is really all about freedom. Remember these words from the prophet Isaiah—words Jesus said described Himself?

> *The Spirit of the Sovereign LORD is on me,*
> *because the LORD has anointed me*
> *to preach good news to the poor.*
> *He has sent me. . .*
> *to proclaim freedom for the captives*
> *and release from darkness for the prisoners,*
> *to proclaim the year of the LORD's favor.*

TIMELINE OF HISTORIC EVENTS FROM AROUND CHRIST'S BIRTH THROUGH THE APOSTLE JOHN'S DEATH

- c. 37 BC–AD 4—Reign of Herod the Great, Roman-appointed King of Judea
- c. 4 BC–AD 6—Rule of Herod Archelaus, ethnarch of Judea, Samaria, and Idumea
- c. 4 BC–AD 39—Rule of Herod Antipas, tetrarch of Galilee and Perea
- c. 4 BC–AD 34—Rule of Herod Philip, tetrarch of Iturea and Trachonitis
- c. 4–6 BC—Birth of Jesus Christ
- c. 2 BC—Birth of Saul of Tarsus (later known as the apostle Paul)
- c. AD 20—Reconstruction of the temple begins
- c. AD 25–28—Ministry of John the Baptist
- c. AD 25–27—Christ's baptism
- c. AD 26–37—Pontius Pilate prefect of Judea
- c. AD 29–30—Christ's crucifixion and resurrection
- c. AD 31–37—Conversion of Saul of Tarsus (the apostle Paul)
- c. AD 31–95—Books of the New Testament written
- c. AD 41—Execution of James by Herod Agrippa I
- c. AD 45–58—The apostle Paul's missionary journeys
- c. AD 49—Roman Emperor Claudius expels Jews from Rome; the church holds the Council of Jerusalem
- c. AD 54—Nero becomes Roman emperor
- c. AD 59–60—Paul's first imprisonment begins
- c. AD 62—Execution of James, the Lord's brother, in Jerusalem
- c. AD 67–68—Paul's final imprisonment and death in Rome
- AD 70—Jerusalem captured by Titus; Herod's temple destroyed
- AD 81—Domitian becomes Roman emperor
- AD 90–100—Persecution of Christians by Domitian
- AD 90–100—Death of the apostle John, the last living apostle

Let's face it: Some of the disciples probably tried the Lord's patience. John, however, is generally regarded as "the disciple whom Jesus loved."

DOES GOD HAVE A SENSE OF HUMOR?

SCRIPTURES REFERENCED:
GENESIS 1:26–27; JAMES 1:13; PSALM 37:13; LUKE 8:40–56; LUKE 6:17–26; JOHN
17:8–19; GALATIANS 5:22–23; NEHEMIAH 8:10; MARK 10:13–16; PROVERBS 17:22

Not every theological debate centers on suffering, sin, or salvation. For some people, the burning question is this: "Does God have a sense of humor?"

POINT, COUNTERPOINT

There's no definitive Bible passage to look to, not even in the oft-quoted book of Hezekiah (you know, that pretend book that always says just what we *want* the Bible to say). So some folks "read between the lines" to support their position. God must have a sense of humor, they say, because He created human beings. With all the crazy things people do, the Lord must enjoy a good chuckle now and then.

A more serious approach to humor, the logical one, goes something like this: Since (a) God created people in His own image, and since (b) people have a sense of humor, then (c) God Himself must have a divine funny bone. Unfortunately, that kind of logic falls apart if you plug different variables into the equation. Since (a) God created people in His own image, and since (b) people like to sin, it certainly *doesn't* follow that (c) God Himself likes to sin. A Bible writer named James was adamant about that: "When tempted, no one should say, 'God is tempting me.' For God cannot be tempted by evil, nor does he tempt anyone."

Still others are nervous about the entire debate. God's holiness, justice, and righteousness, they say, so exceed a trivial thing like a sense of humor that we should simply let the issue rest. But we're already so far into this chapter, we can't stop now.

GIMME A VERSE, PLEASE

Though we mentioned the lack of a *definitive* answer in the Bible, we do find hints of humor here and there. The actual word *humor* appears not a single time in either of the two most popular Bible translations; we do, however, find a handful of references to laughter—even by God Himself.

But we need to be honest here: God's laughter, found three times in the Psalms, really isn't good-natured. What we see is evil men dissing God or hassling righteous people, and God laughing. The thirty-seventh psalm captures His true attitude: "The Lord laughs at the wicked, for he knows their day is coming." That's not the kind of chuckle you'd share with a friend.

So how about Jesus? Surely the human face of God laughed with His disciples, sharing some great "guy moments" with the Twelve, right? If so, none of the New Testament writers thought to jot it down.

We can't say for sure that Jesus Himself laughed, but we know He was once laughed *at*. It happened at the home of Jairus, where the man's twelve-year-old daughter had died. When Jesus told a crowd of mourners, "Stop wailing. . . . She is not dead but asleep," they laughed at Him because they were certain this little girl wouldn't be waking up. But Jesus got the last laugh (if indeed He did laugh) by raising the girl to life and returning her to her astonished parents.

On another occasion, Jesus *talked* about laughter. In a list of blessings and woes, the Lord warned those "who laugh now, for you will mourn and weep." But He also gave laughter a thumbs-up when he encouraged those "who weep now, for you will laugh."

The Lord is often shown in contemplation, or with his face twisted in agony, or with a gentle smile. But how often do you see depictions of Him laughing?

SANCTIFIED SPECULATION

I do believe God has a sense of humor. But I also believe it's a measured part of His being. That would be quite unlike modern society with its constant barrage of blonde jokes, sitcoms, comedy clubs, political speeches, and so on.

Jesus once prayed that His disciples would have "the full measure of my joy within them." That cornucopia of spiritual goodies known as the "fruit of the Spirit" puts joy second on the list—just after love. An old-timer named Nehemiah liked to say, "The joy of the LORD is your strength." It's hard to imagine that kind of joy without laughter.

The fact that children flocked to Jesus seems to argue for a divine sense of humor, too. How many kids do you know who like dour, ever-serious grown-ups?

And then there's the fact that God Himself had Solomon jot down this memorable proverb: "A cheerful heart is good medicine." As with all of scripture, that little gem was recorded for our benefit—we're left to guess if it was written before or after Solomon married a small city's worth of wives (see "Man Marries 700 Women" on page 26).

HUMOR ME

So, go ahead—laugh, love, enjoy life. Yes, God has some serious things to say to us and some serious jobs for us to do. But He's also given us a lot of reason for joy and laughter. And that's no joke.

SOME BIBLE VERSES ABOUT LAUGHTER

- "Abraham fell facedown; he laughed and said to himself, 'Will a son be born to a man a hundred years old? Will Sarah bear a child at the age of ninety?'" (Genesis 17:17).
- "Sarah said, "God has brought me laughter, and everyone who hears about this will laugh with me" (Genesis 21:6).
- "He will yet fill your mouth with laughter and your lips with shouts of joy" (Job 8:21).
- "The One enthroned in heaven laughs; the Lord scoffs at them" (Psalm 2:4).
- "The Lord laughs at the wicked, for he knows their day is coming" (Psalm 37:13).
- "Our mouths were filled with laughter, our tongues with songs of joy. Then it was said among the nations, 'The LORD has done great things for them'" (Psalm 126:2).
- "Even in laughter the heart may ache, and rejoicing may end in grief" (Proverbs 14:13).
- "She [the godly woman] is clothed with strength and dignity; she can laugh at the days to come" (Proverbs 31:25).
- "Laughter," I said, 'is madness. And what does pleasure accomplish?'" (Ecclesiastes 2:2).
- ". . .A time to weep and a time to laugh, a time to mourn and a time to dance" (Ecclesiastes 3:4).
- "Like the crackling of thorns under the pot, so is the laughter of fools" (Ecclesiastes 7:6).
- "A feast is made for laughter, wine makes life merry, and money is the answer for everything" (Ecclesiastes 10:19).
- "Blessed are you who hunger now, for you will be satisfied. Blessed are you who weep now, for you will laugh" (Luke 6:21).
- "Grieve, mourn and wail. Change your laughter to mourning and your joy to gloom" (James 4:9).

NOAH GETS BOMBED

SCRIPTURES REFERENCED:
GENESIS 6–9; EPHESIANS 5:15–16

Sad but true: The last time we see Noah in the Bible, he's bombed, smashed, flat-out drunk.

OUT OF CHARACTER

You'd think that a guy who's 601 years old would know better. Especially when he was introduced to us as "a righteous man, blameless among the people of his time." Noah, the man chosen to build an ark to save his own family and pairs of all the animals from a worldwide flood, was one who "walked faithfully with God."

Up to and during the flood, Noah did everything right, "just as God commanded him." He built a boat that was a football field and a half in length, then rounded up the world's critters for a 150-day cruise (see "How Many Animals on the Ark?" on page 110). When it came time to debark from the ark, Noah basked in God's blessing: "Be fruitful and increase in number and fill the earth."

His seafaring days behind him, Noah returned to his original occupation: farming. Seeds led to vines led to grapes led to wine—which all ultimately led to a very drunk Noah lying naked in his tent. What's up with that?

THEORIES AND CERTAINTIES

Noah's record to this point is so upstanding you have to think this embarrassing episode was an accident. Surely, he wasn't planning to get sloshed. Maybe he was simply surprised by the fermentation of his new jug of grape juice.

The Bible doesn't address that question. What we know for sure is that Noah's son Ham brewed up some big trouble for himself when he found his dad passed out in a tent.

Noah was "uncovered," to use the biblical term, and Ham "saw his father naked." Then he told his two brothers, Shem and Japheth, who used a piece of clothing to cover Noah. But they wouldn't look at their dad in his embarrassing situation—"they walked in backward and covered their father's naked body."

We're left to speculate again as to Ham's motivations, but maybe he thought his dad's situation was funny. When Noah's wine wore off, though, and he learned what had happened, he called down a curse on Ham's family, through Ham's son Canaan: "The lowest of slaves will he be to his brothers."

LAST IMPRESSIONS

Much is said of first impressions, usually with the encouragement to make them good. But Noah's story spotlights the "last impression"—begging the question of how *we* want to be remembered.

In a lifetime of good—950 years' worth—Noah's record includes this one less-than-sterling moment. It's a powerful reminder, as the apostle Paul said, to "Be very careful, then, how you live—not as unwise but as wise. . . because the days are evil."

THE LIFE OF NOAH

- His early life: The Bible is silent about Noah's early life; the first time he is mentioned (when God called him to build the ark and prepare his family for the destruction of the world), he is 500 years old. Noah was the great grandson of Enoch, the man who "walked faithfully with God 300 years" before he was taken to heaven without dying (Genesis 5:22–24; Hebrews 11:5), and the great-great grandson of Methuselah, who lived longer than any man (Genesis 5:25–27), and the son of Lamech (Genesis 5:28–29).
- His family: Noah was married and had three sons—Shem, Ham, and Japheth. The name of Noah's wife is not mentioned in the Bible; she is referred to only as "Noah's wife" (Genesis 6:18; 7:7; 7:13; 8:16; 8:18).
- His call: Noah lived in a time when humans had fallen so far into wickedness that God decided to destroy the world and start over. God called Noah to build an enormous boat—the ark—which would be a temporary home for him, his family, and a certain

A hiker on Turkey's Mount Ararat. Many believe the Bible says Noah's ark landed on this mountain—though the verse actually states "the ark came to rest on the mountains of Ararat" (Genesis 8:4, italics added), indicating it could have been anywhere in the entire mountain range.

number of each member of the animal kingdom. Even though what God commanded him to do seemed strange and humanly impossible, he followed God's instructions to a "T"—despite the fact that he was scoffed at by the unbelievers around him.

- The flood: After Noah completed the ark, gathered all the animals, and entered the ark with his family—his wife and three sons and their wives—God closed the great boat's doors and sent the flood that wiped out every living thing on earth (Genesis 7:16–23). The people and the animals stayed on the ark for several months before the boat came to rest on the mountains of Ararat (Genesis 8:4).

- After the flood: After leaving the ark, Noah built an altar and offered God a sacrifice (Genesis 8:20). God instructed Noah and his family to begin repopulating the earth and also made a covenant with Noah that He would never again destroy the earth with a flood. Noah planted a vineyard and, unfortunately, became drunk. Noah lived 350 years after the flood and died at the ripe old age of 950.

MAN LIVES NEARLY A THOUSAND YEARS

SCRIPTURES REFERENCED:

GENESIS 5; GENESIS 9:29; GENESIS 1:27–31; GENESIS 3:19; GENESIS 6:1–3; DEUTERONOMY 34:5–7; PSALM 90:10; 1 CHRONICLES 29:15; JOB 8:9; JOB 9:25; PSALM 39:5; JAMES 4:14

n our time, a one-hundredth birthday is both a cause for celebration and a minor news event. But early in human history, turning a hundred was rather ho-hum—since people regularly lived seven, eight, or nine times that long.

CHECK THIS OUT

Want specifics? Check out these life spans from the first several generations:

- First generation: Adam, 930 years
- Second generation: Seth, 912 years
- Third generation: Enosh, 905 years
- Fourth generation: Kenan, 910 years
- Fifth generation: Mahalalel, 895 years
- Sixth generation: Jared, 962 years
- Seventh generation: Enoch, 365 years (No, he wasn't a weakling— see "Men Escape Death— Permanently" on page 124.)
- Eighth generation: Methuselah, 969 years
- Ninth generation: Lamech, 777 years
- Tenth generation: Noah, 950 years

The greatest number of candles on any recent birthday cake was 122, for France's Jean Calment. She died shortly thereafter, in 1997, believed to be the world's oldest person at the time. But her lifetime was only one-eighth the length of the Bible's earliest people.

So, what's the deal? Were these guys eating lots of veggies or popping Flintstone vitamins like candy? Noah, who died just fifty years shy of a millennium, had his three sons at age *five hundred*—and was building a 450-foot-long boat (that would be the "ark") a century after that.

Moses, in his eighties—and needing some help to keep his arms raised over the Israelite army as it fought the Amalekites. "As long as Moses held up his hands, the Israelites were winning, but whenever he lowered his hands, the Amalekites were winning" (Exodus 17:11). Moses' brother Aaron and a man named Hur kept the old leader's arms elevated.

THE LONG AND SHORT OF IT

The Bible doesn't clearly explain those looong lives in earth's early days, but we might read between the lines for some clues. Adam, of course, was made directly by God, part of that "very good" creation recorded in Genesis 1. Apparently, Adam had been designed to live forever—because part of the curse for his sin was that he would die ("for dust you are and to dust you will return"). The curse would apply to every child, grandchild, great-grandchild, and so on, down Adam's line—including you and me. Sorry to be the bearer of that bad news.

Anyway, Adam's sin touched off an aging process that soon cut the human life span from infinity to about 900 years. By the time of the great flood, God—disgusted with the world's complete sinfulness—decreed a new human life span of 120 years.

That's exactly how long Moses lived, though he wrote in a psalm (number 90) that "our days may come to seventy

EDEN: THE PERFECT ETERNAL HOME, UNTIL. . .

The world's first human beings—Adam and his wife, Eve—have the distinction of never having been born. . .at least in the biological sense. God created these two people and placed them in the Garden of Eden, a beautiful—make that *perfect*—place filled with pleasant trees and plants for food. God made the animals, placed them in the garden, and instructed Adam to name them.

The couple were to care for Eden, and had free run of the garden, but were commanded not to eat of "the tree of the knowledge of good and evil." When they listened to the serpent (actually the devil in snake's clothing) and disobeyed God's command, sin entered into what was to be a perfect picture of fellowship between God and His creation.

The immediate consequences of Adam and Eve's sin are listed in Genesis 3:10–24:

- They were now ashamed and afraid of God.
- Eve would suffer during childbirth.
- Adam would labor to work the ground God had cursed.
- They would experience physical death.
- Eve would desire for her husband and be ruled over by him.

years, or eighty, if our strength endures." However many years we may live, Moses noted, "they quickly pass."

BLINK, AND YOU MAY MISS IT

The brevity and fragility of life is a common theme in the Bible: "Our days on earth are but a shadow"; "My days are swifter than a runner"; "You have

OLDEST PEOPLE IN THE BIBLE

- Methuselah (969 years, Genesis 5:27)
- Jared (962 years, Genesis 5:20)
- Noah (950 years, Genesis 9:29)
- Adam (930 years, Genesis 5:5)
- Seth (912 years, Genesis 5:8)
- Kenan (910 years, Genesis 5:14)
- Enosh (905 years, Genesis 5:11)
- Mahalalel (895 years, Genesis 5:17)
- Lamech (777 years, Genesis 5:31)
- Shem (600 years, Genesis 11:10–11)
- Eber (464 years, Genesis 11:16–17)
- Arphaxad (438 years, Genesis 11:12–13)
- Salah (433 years, Genesis 11:14–15)
- Enoch (365 years, Genesis 5:23–24)
- Peleg (239 years, Genesis 11:18–19)
- Reu (239 years, Genesis 11:20–21)
- Serug (230 years, Genesis 11:22–23)
- Terah (205 years, Genesis 11:32)
- Isaac (180 years, Genesis 35:28)
- Abraham (175 years, Genesis 25:7)
- Nahor (148 years, Genesis 11:24–25)
- Jacob (147 years, Genesis 47:28)
- Amram (137 years, Exodus 6:20)
- Ishmael (137 years, Genesis 25:17)
- Levi (137 years, Exodus 6:16)
- Kohath (133 years, Exodus 6:18)
- Jehoiada (130 years, 2 Chronicles 24:15)
- Sarah (127 years, Genesis 23:1)
- Aaron (123 years, Numbers 33:39)
- Moses (120 years, Deuteronomy 34:7)
- Joseph (110 years, Genesis 50:22)
- Joshua (110 years, Judges 2:8)

made my days a mere handbreadth"; "What is your life? You are a mist that appears for a little while and then vanishes."

While that thought may be a downer, there is good news: it is possible to live forever. And that just may be the Bible's greatest curiosity of all. Please read on. . . .

MAN LIVES FOREVER

SCRIPTURES REFERENCED:

REVELATION 22:13; JOHN 10:27–28; 1 CORINTHIANS 15:42–44; JOHN 3:16; EPHESIANS 2:8–9; ROMANS 10:9; LUKE 5:31; MARK 9:42–49; ROMANS 5:8

If Methuselah were alive today, *The Guinness Book of World Records* would beat a path to his door. His 969-year life span would certainly warrant a mention among all those other superlatives: the longest fingernails, the most consecutive jumps on a pogo stick, the biggest pumpkin pie, and so on and so on.

But, truth be told, Methuselah's a real piker when it comes to length of days. People can actually live forever.

LIFE OF A DIFFERENT SORT

No, we haven't discovered Ponce de Leon's illusive fountain of youth. And despite the claims of cosmetic companies, there's really no such thing as an "antiaging" cream.

Since this book is all about the Bible, we turn to the Bible to find eternal life. And, appropriately, *Bible Curiosities* closes as it opened: with Jesus Christ. (He did call Himself "the Beginning and the End," you know.)

"My sheep listen to my voice; I know them, and they follow me," Jesus once said. "I give them eternal life, and they shall never perish."

That's great news, but even better news is that we won't be stuck in our aging bodies, which, though we don't like to consider it, begin dying the day we're born. When Jesus promises you eternal life, it comes with a sleek new version of your body, one designed to run forever. "The body that is sown [buried] is perishable, it is raised imperishable," the apostle Paul wrote to Christians in Corinth; "it is sown in dishonor, it is raised in glory; it is sown in weakness, it is raised in power; it is sown a natural body, it is raised a spiritual body."

JESUS' OWN WORDS TEACHING SALVATION THROUGH FAITH IN HIM

- "And as Moses lifted up the bronze snake on a pole in the wilderness, so the Son of Man must be lifted up, so that everyone who believes in him will have eternal life" (John 3:14–15 NLT).
- "For God so loved the world, that he gave his only begotten Son, that whosoever believeth in him should not perish, but have everlasting life" (John 3:16 KJV).
- "Whoever believes in the Son has eternal life, but whoever rejects the Son will not see life, for God's wrath remains on them" (John 3:36).
- "Very truly I tell you, whoever hears my word and believes him who sent me has eternal life and will not be judged but has crossed over from death to life" (John 5:24).
- "Then they said to Him, 'What shall we do, that we may work the works of God?' Jesus answered and said to them, 'This is the work of God, that you believe in Him whom He sent'" (John 6:28–29 NKJV).
- "I am the resurrection and the life. He who believes in Me, though he may die, he shall live. And whoever lives and believes in Me shall never die" (John 11:25–26 NKJV).

WHAT WOULD YOU PAY?

To live forever in a perfect body—now that's something special. But what does it cost?

Jesus Himself answered that question in perhaps the most familiar of all scriptures—that classic reference that even gets national television airtime during extra-point kicks at football games. John 3:16 says,

> *For God so loved the world that he gave his one and only Son, that whoever believes in him shall not perish but have eternal life.*

What? You just have to believe? That seems way too easy—there must be a catch.

Not according to our old friend Paul the apostle. "It is by grace you have been saved, through faith," he told the church in Ephesus, "and this is not from yourselves, it is the gift of God—not by works, so that no one can boast." Paul gave the entire "plan of salvation" in a nutshell in his letter to Roman believers: "If you declare with your mouth, 'Jesus is Lord,' and believe in your heart that God raised him from the dead, you will be saved."

Simple, isn't it? Almost shockingly so.

EVEN MORE SHOCKING. . .

And guess what? This forever life is not only free, it's available to absolutely everyone.

Salvation isn't just for the "nice" people, the "moral" people, or the "at least I'm better than she is" people. Jesus Himself ran with a pretty rough crowd sometimes, saying, "It is not the healthy who need a doctor, but the sick." Sin makes us "sick," and every last one of us is a sinner, according to Romans 3:23. Skip ahead three chapters, to Romans 6:23, to find the results of our spiritual health care crisis: "The wages of sin is death." And that death is the door to a fiery punishment in hell.

If you stop there, the picture is bleak. But there's a second half to Romans 6:23, a dozen words that promise enormous hope: "The gift of God is eternal life in Christ Jesus our Lord."

Think about that—it's the single most stunning aspect of the entire Bible, far beyond the multiplying of food, the parting of seas, or even the reversing of our earth's rotation. A perfect and holy God, who demands death as punishment for sin, offers never-ending life to sinners. Why? Because His equally perfect and holy Son, Jesus Christ, took our punishment when He died on the cross.

HE LOVES YOU, YEAH, YEAH, YEAH

When the Beatles sang, "All You Need Is Love," they put a real truth to music. Well, maybe a half-truth.

The mop tops' warm, fuzzy, "let's all feel good about each other" kind of love may have its place, but what we really *need* is God's love—which takes the very human form of Jesus Christ. "God demonstrates his own love for us in this," Paul wrote to the Romans: "While we were still sinners, Christ died for us."

So there's your biggest, baddest Bible curiosity of all. You can marvel in stunned silence, whoop in the joy of victory, or laugh in giddy relief.

Whatever you do, *believe* it.

"God demonstrates his own love for us in this: While we were still sinners, Christ died for us" (Romans 5:8).

THE NATIONS
AT PENTECOST

PLACE Location represented
at Pentecost according
to Acts 2

Roman Empire

Parthian Empire

Peter preaches at the
Temple at Pentecost

Copyright © 2007 by Barbour Publishing,

NEW TESTAMENT FAITH IN JESUS

- About 3,000 people in Jerusalem on the day of Pentecost (Acts 2:41)
- More than 5,000 people in Jerusalem (Acts 4:4)
- Unnamed multitudes (Acts 5:14)
- The crippled man at Lystra (Acts 14:8–10)
- Stephen (Acts 6:8)
- The Ethiopian eunuch (Acts 8:37)
- Aeneas (Acts 9:34)
- The people of Lydda and Sharon (Acts 9:35)
- The people of Joppa (Acts 9:42)

- The people of Antioch (Acts 11:20–21)
- Sergius Paulus (Acts 13:12)
- Eunice, Lois, and Timothy (Acts 16:1)
- Lydia (Acts 16:14)
- The Philippian jailer and his family (Acts 16:31–34)
- Crispus and others in Corinth (Acts 18:8)
- Jews at Rome (Acts 28:23–24)
- The Ephesians (Ephesians 1:13–14)
- The Colossians (Colossians 1:2–4)
- The Thessalonians (1 Thessalonians 1:6)
- Philemon (Philemon 4–5)

INDEX

ART CREDITS

Unless otherwise noted, all images are licensed from Shutterstock.